AUTHENTIC INCLUSION™

AUTHENTIC INCLUSION™

Drives Disruptive Innovation

Frances West

Printed in the United States of America.
Library of Congress Control Number: 2018965296
ISBN: 978-1-949639-34-6

TO MY PARENTS, SHU-MING WANG AND MAN-YUEN LIU,
WHO GAVE ME LIFE

TO MY HUSBAND, CHIP, WHO GIVES ME LOVE

TO MY SONS, HAN AND BION, WHO GIVE ME PURPOSE

AND

TO PJ EDINGTON AND MY LUU, FORMER IBM
COLLEAGUES WHO PASSED AWAY DURING THEIR
PRIME AND GAVE ME MOTIVATION

TABLE OF CONTENTS

AUTHENTIC INCLUSION™

The institutional insight that human diversity is at the core of disruptive innovation. It calls for holistic actions across all parts of an institution to respect an individual human's ability to make a difference not in spite of, but because of, their difference. By putting humans first, prosperity can have longevity because principle, purpose, and profit are harmoniously aligned.

CHAPTER 1
What Is Authentic Inclusion and Why Is It a Business Imperative?

Difference has value. This is not a new concept. Whether it's in the form of a new line of thinking, an external perspective, or an unconventional action, getting "outside of the box" is a tried-and-true method to generate new energy and ideas. Difference creates synergy. It promotes understanding. It fuels creativity and innovation. And because we live in a world full of differences—different abilities, ages, and cultural backgrounds, to name just a few—it only makes sense that our lives reflect these differences.

I could spend many pages talking about how difference is beneficial in a general sense, but you've almost certainly heard it before. People are discussing the importance of diversity and inclusion in every facet of society. What I would like to focus on is how those elements play out in a business context, and more specifically, in the tech world. As IBM's first Chief Accessibility Officer; working with people with disabilities firsthand for over a decade; and a longtime specialist in digital inclusion, innovation, and accessibility, tech is where I have the most to say.

The synergy, understanding, and innovation that difference promotes are essential in the tech world—and in the business world at large. As such, we must find ways not just to acknowledge its worth but to harness it effectively. In other words, we must embrace Authentic Inclusion™.

WHAT IS AUTHENTIC INCLUSION?

Authentic Inclusion, as I define it within the business realm, is the institutional insight that human diversity is at the core of disruptive innovation. It calls for holistic actions across all parts of an organization to respect an individual human's ability to make a difference, not in spite of, but *because of,* their difference. By putting humans first, prosperity can have longevity because principle, purpose, and profit are harmoniously aligned.

As I mentioned, this is not a new idea. Numerous studies and articles have addressed the subject over the past decade. The authors of a 2013 *Harvard Business Review* article, "How Diversity Can Drive Innovation," wrote, "New research provides compelling evidence that diversity unlocks innovation and drives market growth—a finding that should intensify efforts to ensure that executive ranks both embody and embrace the power of differences."[1]

And in 2017, *Forbes* published a study, "Fostering Innovation Through a Diverse Workforce," which stated, "Diversity is a key driver of innovation and is a critical component of being successful on a global scale. Senior executives are recognizing that a diverse set of experiences, perspectives, and backgrounds is crucial to innovation

---

1   Sylvia Ann Hewlett, Melinda Marshall, and Laura Sherbin, "How Diversity Can Drive Innovation," *Harvard Business Review*, December 2013, https://hbr.org/2013/12/how-diversity-can-drive-innovation.

and the development of new ideas."[2]

A simple Google search on "diversity and innovation" will return many results with articles like those quoted above. And yet, anyone who has read the news lately is also aware of the diversity problems in the tech world—problems that have led to high-profile harassment and discrimination lawsuits at some of Silicon Valley's biggest companies. I could list them here, but that doesn't seem productive. This issue goes well beyond a few specific companies; it's part of a broader culture. And, unfortunately, there will probably be more of these lawsuits before the problem is solved. Moreover, it indicates that, despite the fact that we know diversity is good for business, our practices don't really reflect that.

So, where is the disconnect? Why aren't all the smart, influential people leading the tech sector embracing Authentic Inclusion in their companies with a sense of urgency? I've heard a number of answers to that question: *It's too expensive . . . The ROI is too difficult to calculate . . . We hired a consultant to help us figure that out . . .* and so on.

It's a complex issue, to be sure. Changing a company's culture and operation is not a simple task—especially when it's been ingrained over the years, and when the industry at large maintains the same perspective and practices. But it's not something that anyone can afford to ignore. Without Authentic Inclusion, companies risk many things—from a lack of innovation to brand damage—all of which stand to have a negative impact on profits.

WHAT IS IT NOT?

Authentic Inclusion is not a general inclusion discussion. There are plenty of people out there talking about inclusion. The discussion I want to

---

2   "Fostering Innovation Through a Diverse Workforce," *Forbes* Insights, 2017, https://images.forbes.com/forbesinsights/StudyPDFs/Innovation_Through_Diversity.pdf.

have is anchored in the business world: the institutional practice of placing diversity at the heart of operations and innovation.

It's not charity. There's nothing wrong with approaching something with an attitude of empathy, or wanting to "help" someone. But that's not what this is about. Authentic Inclusion is a holistic business practice that can lead to growth and longevity for your company.

It is not something that can be outsourced or assigned to a single department, such as Human Resources. This needs to be embraced companywide, starting with buy-in from the people at the top. If those in the boardroom and the executive suite are not involved, there is very little chance that a company will be able to effect this kind of broad, cultural, and business process transformation.

It's not just about people—it's also about technology. Of course, you are investing in diverse talent when you hire. But you must also invest in the technology necessary to support, enable, and adapt to everyone you bring on board.

It's not something you can afford to ignore. If you want disruptive innovation—as opposed to just incremental progress—you need to have very diverse thinkers and workers in your company. People often argue that it costs too much money to do this. But the fact is, if you factor these things in from the beginning, then it won't cost you "extra"—it will simply be part of the fabric of your business.

It's not something best dealt with in crisis mode. Without the proactive, embedded principles of an inclusive-thinking practice, operation, and organization, companies open themselves up to scandals, lawsuits, and brand damage. Then, they will often try to solve the problem by throwing money at it through consultants, studies, and new positions. There is nothing wrong with these additions, in and of themselves. But if you can establish Authentic Inclusion as a foundation of your company early on, you can avoid the long-term effects of catastrophes like public lawsuits in the first place.

It's not just about people with disabilities. My experience in working as Chief Accessibility Officer with a primary focus on enabling people with disabilities and the aging to achieve parity gave me the insight that this is about humanity in general.

WHY IS IT SO IMPORTANT NOW?

From the smartphones in our pockets to the artificial intelligence being developed for nearly every purpose imaginable, it is hard to deny that technology is becoming a critical part of human existence. I believe that within the span of the next decade, any human job that that can be codified has the potential to be replaced by artificial intelligence.

I am not talking about a dystopian future of warring robots. I am talking about the steady and inevitable growth of technology that's happening now, and at a very swift pace. The struggle to find harmony between technology and humanity is going to become a very real issue.

We are already seeing it crop up in our culture—from smartphone addiction, fake news, and online bullying, to job application sites that preemptively exclude blind applicants. The longer we ignore the human aspects of technology, from its development to its usage, the greater a disadvantage we are creating for humanity.

So, as the machines become smarter and more human-like, the humans must become more human to manage or outsmart the machines. And in the tech sector, in particular, it's crucial that in the race to innovate, companies do not lose sight of humanity. After all, the main purpose of technology is to solve human problems, right? If we were to hashtag this imperative, it would be #HumanFirst.

We need to consider the human attributes that a machine cannot codify as easily—things like creativity, empathy, and collaboration—or character traits like persistence and grit. What we consider to be "soft skills" are going to become some of the most critical proficiencies for managing technology, especially at the AI level. This is why Authentic Inclusion is both urgent and crucial.

TECHNOLOGY MADE HUMAN

My understanding of Authentic Inclusion has grown throughout my career as I dealt with inclusion challenges in the business and tech worlds for over three decades. During my last job at IBM, I worked to solve the issues faced by people with disabilities or different abilities in our workforce. I've come to see that people's productivity and quality of life can be significantly improved or hindered by their interactions with technology. People who do not fit the standard mold can be completely barred from participation if technology is not part of the thinking from the start. But when it's taken into account, they can be empowered to add tremendous value. To factor in the human experience, we must consider its breadth and depth and include diverse voices in the conversation and actions.

For instance, my own experience getting older has driven home a statistical reality: our population is aging. A large generation of people with years of accumulated knowledge and expertise—and the aging bodies that come with that—will have needs to accommodate. If your company has embraced a philosophy of Authentic Inclusion, then you will already have the infrastructure and culture necessary to enable aging employees to continue working productively. And because you have the infrastructure and understanding in place already, you can leverage them to serve your aging customers—a double win.

It's obvious, but still bears saying: no one is exempt from the aging process. And as the retirement age continues to rise, more accommodations will be necessary for all of us. This is just a fact of life.

As a naturalized American citizen, I am also keenly aware of the potential for America's role in the charge to humanize our approach to technology. America was built on a foundation of innovation and differences. People from all over the world—myself included—have come here over the decades and centuries, to make a life and take part in the American Dream. If any country is going to be a leader in Authentic Inclusion, it should be the United States.

That's not to say that Authentic Inclusion is solely an American idea. The concept is relevant anywhere in the world that businesses exist. But I believe that the US should own it.

The US has the foundation—from the Bill of Rights to the Constitution—supporting the idea that everybody should be equal. I don't want to sound too idealistic, but I truly believe that the US can and should be a moral leader in this area. Supporting people's differences for the sake of innovation and profitability seems to me like a distinctly American notion.

In the chapters to come, we'll discuss the future of innovation and profitability—topics that concern all of us in the business realm—and how they can be achieved through Authentic Inclusion. I hope these ideas will resonate with you.

To begin, I will tell you more about what led me to this subject and how I came to understand just how vital Authentic Inclusion can be.

CHAPTER 2
How Diversity Shapes Human Experience: My Life, My Journey

I was born in Taiwan, my parents' middle child and their only daughter. My mother was a traditional Chinese woman who followed the traditional thinking that a young woman's best option was to find a wealthy husband by looking good. She tried to make me conform to this cultural norm, but she always said I was different—that I took after my dad more than my brothers did.

My father was a mechanical engineer who got his start in the Chinese Navy in the 1940s. He was one of the first engineers to be sent to Miami to learn how to operate the US Navy's ships. He returned to China bearing souvenirs like Coca-Cola and Wrigley's Spearmint gum—and a deep interest in other cultures, something I acquired from him.

Eventually, he became an advisor to the United Nations in Taiwan in the late 1960s. He worked on maritime development projects and essentially trained young men and sailors to become merchant marines. Because my father had shipping expertise, had received engineering training in the US, and had learned English, he was one of the few people with the right skills and knowledge to work on these programs.

During holidays like Christmas, my father would invite his UN colleagues to our house. They taught us about Western customs and etiquette, like how to decorate a Christmas tree, how to eat with a fork and knife, and how to say certain English phrases, such as, "You talk too much." I was fascinated with our visitors from faraway places and all their customs.

I was also very interested in school and learning, much to my mother's chagrin. I was always among the top three students in my class, and when I would bring home my certificate, my mom would say things like, "Oh, another piece of toilet paper." Meanwhile, my brother, barely a B student, was praised for his efforts. When I look back, her intention wasn't to be cruel. Rather, she wanted to bring me back into alignment with typical gender expectations in Chinese culture at the time. Academic achievement was fine, but it shouldn't overshadow my prospects for finding a suitable husband.

At that moment, it didn't feel fair, of course, but rather than being bitter about her reaction, I figured I must not be doing enough, and I would just have to work harder. Instead of men or makeup, I continued to pursue academic excellence.

Despite her seeming disinterest in my grades, my mother was never stingy about ensuring I had the best education available. She sent me to a girls' Christian boarding school in Taiwan that was competitive and expensive—much like the private schools in the US. It was during that time that I started to become more aware of my differences. For one, I was very tall for a Chinese girl. This made me stand out in a way that was not always welcome. In school plays, for instance, I would be cast in the role of a man—or a tree. Rather than pout that I would never be cast as the princess, I accepted those roles; I chose to be the tree. I didn't want to be left out. And at the end of the day, I was still in the school play. I still had the experience of being on stage and the joy of participating. I was still part of the cast.

A CULTURE CLASH IN HONG KONG

In 1971, the UN made the People's Republic of China a member, ousting Taiwan. As a result of this change, my father lost his job and had to scramble to find a new one. Eventually, he was offered a position in Hong Kong, at the Worldwide Shipping Company, and our family was required to relocate.

The move to Hong Kong was a difficult transition for all of us. For one thing, having lived in Taiwan, we spoke Mandarin. In the British colony of Hong Kong, people spoke English and Cantonese. Though my father spoke English, the rest of us did not. Due to the language barrier, my mother could barely purchase groceries.

I have a vivid memory from that summer of my mother sitting under a banyan tree, crying. "What am I going to do with the three of you?" she said. My brothers and I had been in the best private schools in Taiwan. Now, overnight, we couldn't even pass an entrance exam—not only because we didn't speak English or Cantonese but also because we hadn't studied the right subjects. In Taiwan, we had been taught modern Chinese literature, whereas, in Hong Kong, students were taught classic Chinese literature. I saw firsthand how a shift in culture, expectations, and environment could have a huge impact on our perceived ability and worth.

When we finally did start school, we experienced what you might call a culture clash. The other students wanted nothing to do with my brothers and me, and when I came home each day in tears, my mom would tell me, "If you do well in school, you will become popular." So I buckled down and tried to learn as much as I could. This about-face encouragement from my mother may seem surprising, but the Chinese at base are very pragmatic, and she recognized a social opportunity for me through good grades. And, in a way, my mother knew by then that I would not conform to traditional Chinese gender norms.

When it came time for college, I was accepted at both the University of Hong Kong and the Chinese University of Hong Kong. I chose the Chinese University of Hong Kong because it follows the four-year undergraduate university system. In my second semester of college, I saw a flyer about an exchange program to the US; the organizers would be conducting interviews on campus soon. I never thought I would get in—my grades had slipped because I was having too much fun—but I decided to interview anyway so I could practice my English conversational skills.

Three professors—two American and one Chinese—asked me questions like, "Why do you want to go to United States?" I gave the best generic answers I could think of. Then they asked me what I would do if I found my roommate smoking marijuana. I thought it was an odd question. Rather than give a serious, textbook answer, which is more typical of a diligent Chinese student, I told them, "Oh, I wouldn't partake in their smoking, but it's their country . . . and I guess they can do whatever they want." I got the feeling that the American professors liked my answer.

I never expected to hear from them again, but two weeks later they called to tell me I had gotten in. When it was time to go, I had two schools to choose from: University of Redlands in California, and Washington and Lee University in Virginia. I chose Washington and Lee because it was closer to Washington, DC, and New York City. I just wanted to see that part of the country. I knew very little about the American South—and I definitely did not know Washington and Lee was an all-male school.

FREE TO BE ME IN THE US

That fall, I flew to New York City and boarded a Greyhound bus to Lexington, Virginia. A professor named Dr. Goldsten and his wife had agreed to serve as my host family.

The Goldsten family was incredibly welcoming and generous from the start. They took me in, gave me my own bedroom—something I had never had before—and included me in all their family traditions. I celebrated Hanukkah and Passover with them and learned how to make blintzes and matzo-ball soup. (I also gained thirteen pounds that year.) They also helped me through the ins and outs of college life, giving advice along the way.

As one of five women on campus, I had to carry a handmade sign to put on the bathroom door when I used it—the campus had no women's bathrooms at the time. I was nineteen and adventurous, and I didn't think anything of it. I was loving the entire experience, and after a few months, I decided that I wanted to stay. Here, unlike the universities in Hong Kong, I could take any course I wanted.

Because I was far away from my parents' ideas about what I should be doing—and from the restricted path of the Chinese universities—I was able to explore my interests to my heart's content. American literature, TV production, geology—I took any class that sounded interesting to me. It was a liberating feeling, having the freedom of choice.

I also loved my new group of friends—young women who were also exchange students from other countries. That year, one of my friends threw a Christmas party, and that is where I met my husband. He was a young, Southern man who walked up to me and introduced himself as Chip. I introduced myself as Frances Wang, speaking with the British accent I had from my education in Hong Kong.

"Chip?" I said. "Like potato chip?"

"No, like chocolate chip," he replied. Somehow, I knew this would be something.

Meanwhile, my parents were unhappy that I'd decided to stay in the US. I was being disloyal, they said, and withdrew their financial support. I was not happy about their reaction, but I was determined to make my new plan work—with or without their help. I took Dr. Goldsten's advice and applied to a state school, which would be more affordable. Luckily, I already had my F1 student visa, so all I had to do was get accepted somewhere. According to Dr. Goldsten, the University of Kentucky in Lexington had a good business program, so I applied there and was accepted.

Determined to take care of myself and graduate from college, I applied for a scholarship and took a job in the university canteen, working a few hours around lunchtime each day. Not only did I make enough to pay my rent, I also learned some valuable lessons. I witnessed a great deal of mismanagement and discrimination working in that kitchen alongside the mostly African-American staff.

I watched the disrespectful and dismissive treatment of my black coworkers. I saw the hugely unfair and dysfunctional power differential between management and low-level employees. I knew it was wrong on a number of levels. Though I didn't experience the same type of harassment, I felt the weight of it.

Most likely, it was this experience that seeded my ideas about Authentic Inclusion—and shaped my current leadership and management style. Over the years, I've had mentors tell me that I'm paying too much attention to my team and not enough to the "people upstairs"—the ones in positions to set the course for the company and impact one's career trajectory. But to me, paying attention to the working team is a key part of the Authentic Inclusion philosophy.

#HUMANFIRST, BEFORE THE ADVENT OF THE HASHTAG

Things were on track: I had earned good grades and was getting ready to graduate, and Chip and I were engaged.

At the end of my last semester, in the spring of 1979, I had an on-campus interview with an IBM recruiter. Applicants were supposed to be US residents, and I had none of the qualifications—not to mention the fact that my English was still somewhat broken at the time and my work experience was limited—but I chose to ignore all that. My grades were good, after all, and I just wanted to talk to the man. I figured that, no matter what happened, at least I'd learn something. During the interview, I found creative ways to spin the importance of the jobs I'd had to date (working in the university canteen, waitressing in a Chinese restaurant and a Ramada Inn, and licking stamps in the mailroom of a bank).

The interviewer, a man named Frank Friedersdorf, listened carefully as I explained my work experience and my views on customer service. At the end of the interview, I told him that I didn't have a green card (permanent resident card) yet, but that I was about to be married to a US citizen. At the end of our meeting, Frank said, "You know what, Frances? You have a job with IBM. Go get married, have a great honeymoon, and when you come back, you can start with IBM."

When I told people about my job offer, nobody believed me. Why would a company like IBM give someone like me a job? Once I convinced people it was true, they immediately assumed it was a sec-retarial position. But for whatever reason, after talking with me, Frank had decided I was going to be a systems engineer. As a marketing major, I'd never taken a single engineering or programming course, but—much like my decision to take on the role of "Tree" in the school play, or attend an all-male college—I thought, "Well, I better just say 'yes' and figure this out later."

Though we only met a couple of times, Frank Friedersdorf became an important figure in my history. He had broken every rule in the book by hiring me. He clearly was not working from a standard checklist during our interview—but rather from a human level. I will always be grateful to him for seeing my potential as a person and giving me a big chance. It definitely paid off; I went on to have a decades-long career at IBM, a company that I later learned was actually a pioneer in inclusion and accessibility. Hashtags weren't a thing at the time, but Frank's actions were definitely early signs of the human-first philosophy.

MARRY THE CHICKEN, FOLLOW THE CHICKEN

There is an old Chinese saying, "Marry the chicken, follow the chicken. Marry the dog, follow the dog." Over the years, Chip and I have both played the role of the chicken or the dog, following each other wherever our careers took us. In 1980, Chip was starting a Ph.D. program in psychology at Michigan State University in East Lansing, and after a year at IBM in Kentucky, I transferred to the company's Grand Rapids office to work as a systems engineer in the data processing division.

Grand Rapids is where my professional life really began. My accounts included a number of hard-core manufacturers—tank engine and iron-casting companies. You can just imagine the creativity and tenacity it took for me to be effective in my job; here I was, an Asian girl in her early twenties, walking through a shop floor full of white men and trying to give the IT managers (all white men) advice about how to implement or upgrade their System 370 mainframe computers—which cost four to five million dollars each.

What I found in those early days was that the men in the technology business could be very open and engaging if you made an effort to bond with them over a common topic of interest. I did some research and found out that most Michigan men liked fishing and hunting. So in between debugging the COBOL programs, I would bring up questions like, *How do you do ice fishing in the winter?* Or *How do you store deer meat?* A little extra effort on my part enabled me to bridge differences of age, gender, and race and allowed us to connect on a human level.

After a few years in Michigan, I would routinely get smoked steelhead trout or cured venison as gifts from my customers. Those early experiences in a workplace dominated by white men taught me what I needed to do to make meaningful connections and prepared me for the future.

Our next move was to Boston for Chip's pre- and postdoctoral internship years at Harvard. I became a systems engineer manager in IBM's Boston branch, working on accounts in manufacturing, health care, higher education, and retail. My first son was born in 1985, and my second son four years later. To be a working mom in those days was both exciting and challenging—exciting because companies were just beginning to provide services to women in the workforce. IBM's progressive maternity leave and childcare policies really won the hearts and minds of many women workers, including myself. Our respect and loyalty to the company were rooted in these human-first policies, beyond pay or promotion. But life was also challenging because there was no roadmap. Working mothers had to figure things out as they went.

Any working parent will tell you how hard it is to "have it all." But I was determined. I wanted a strong family and a strong career.

As a tiger mom with a demanding job, it was not easy to find balance. Looking back, I could never have accomplished what I did without a strong support system in place—and the two key pillars were my husband and my mom. Chip was flexible with his working hours because of his job as a clinical psychologist, and my mother moved in full time after my father died in 1984 to help raise the family—all the way up until 2011, the year she passed away.

A CULTURAL BARRIER IN MY OWN COUNTRY

Though it changed the world with the invention of the PC and was ranked as the world's most admired company for many years, IBM was not immune to technology changes and market forces. In the early 1990s, the rapid rise of rival personal computer companies put a big dent in IBM's legacy mainframe business. By the end of 1993, IBM was in rough shape and facing major layoffs. I had just been promoted to my dream job as manager of the RISC 6000 Fighter Pilot team—but I had to turn around and lay off top-notch employees.

The experience was incredibly difficult, but it was made easier because IBM's human resources and senior management teams were compassionate and transparent. They communicated frequently and openly about the challenge we faced as a company and asked all IBMers around the world to pull together. And we did. We did it because our new leader, Lou Gerstner, was clear about what he wanted for the employees and for the company. We did it also because we were a team. What this lesson taught me, till this day, is that if a leader at the top is able to communicate in an authentically human way, the troops will respond, regardless of how difficult the circumstances may be.

As IBM US was going through a tough transition, the need for computers in emerging markets such as China was growing. In early

1994, I decided to take a position with IBM China, where I stayed for the next three years as an overseas assignee in Beijing. At first, I thought it would be easy—like going home. I spoke the language, I had solid business training, and I'd already been a manager at IBM US. I bought some nice new clothes, packed up my family and our cat, Mei Mei, and moved to Beijing.

The job in China turned out to be the most profoundly challenging three years of my life. What I hadn't realized was that all my thinking and business instincts had been honed in the US, and this was indeed a "foreign" assignment.

Doing business in China was a completely different experience. Because it was a sales job, it was important to be able to "read" customers to close deals. Even though I was carrying on all my conversations in Chinese, I was missing much of the nuance. I would have to count on my local sales rep to give me the lowdown. I would excuse myself from meetings, sneaking into the hallway to call the rep and ask, "What is he implying? What is he talking about?" He would help me interpret the subtle messages the customers were sending us and figure out whether they were really interested in buying or negotiating. Six months into the assignment, I was completely beaten down because I could not read my customers.

Up to that point, I had always said to my psychologist husband, "I don't need your services. I'm Chinese. I'm tough." I would joke that therapy was not for me, telling him, "I'm a strong and balanced person." But six months into my China assignment, I came home, crawled onto the couch, and told my husband that I was experiencing an identity crisis. Even though I *was* Chinese, I no longer *felt* Chinese. I had realized that, at least in a business sense, I was actually an American.

Over time, I was able to understand what the customers were

implying, but along the way I learned a hard-earned lesson: you cannot be too presumptuous or overconfident about your ability to comprehend another person—even if you are literally speaking the same language. You have to be prepared to question your assumptions, open yourself up to new input, and ask for help.

One more unexpected lesson I learned was that, in China, even the discrimination was different. Up to that point, the primary discrimination I had faced was based on race. Over the years, I had to deal with both overt and subtle discriminatory attitudes against Asians here and there. I developed strategies to deal with these situations, such as using humor to address the issue, calling out moments of bias and mocking them to neutralize the tension—and ultimately getting someone to see eye-to-eye with me.

But here, the issue was not ethnicity; it was more about gender. At the time, a lot of expats were moving to China for all kinds of business. Managers were coming in from Taiwan, Singapore, from Hong Kong—all Chinese, like me—but almost none were female.

When my manager—an American named Del Davis—had interviewed me for the position, he inquired about all of my business credentials, and then said, "Here are my final three questions: Can you smoke? Can you sing? And can you drink?"

I had been surprised by the questions, but as it turned out, they were pertinent to my customer-facing sales job. At that time in China, everybody smoked, drinking often took place at events, and karaoke was a huge part of the business culture. I later found out that—in addition to drinking, smoking, and singing—as a woman, I was also expected to dance with clients from time to time.

Given that the Asian business culture is very male-centric, the attitude toward women can be unsettling. There were occasions where my male colleagues would ask me to join them for lunch, and then they would sit there and crack inappropriate jokes. When I brought up business strategy, they would just look at me, puzzled, and walk away, not comfortable or capable of carrying on a business discussion with a woman.

Though it took a tremendous amount of energy and focus, I was able to forge ahead and get my work done. It was 1994, and China was just developing its banking system. Along with what I consider to be among my biggest achievements—helping China build its interbank payment system (the Chinese equivalent of the Federal Reserve) and the Shanghai Stock Exchange's brokerage system—I was also building an important foundation for my future work in accessibility and inclusion. Those three years were difficult, but they also helped me to develop a keen awareness of and empathy for others working under unaccommodating circumstances.

FINDING MY WAY TO ACCESSIBILITY

After three years in Beijing, it was time to return to the US. I held several executive positions at IBM over the next six years, working in the insurance industry, global services, and with IBM Lotus. And then in 2003, I took a position as the director of IBM's Human Ability and Accessibility Center, which ultimately led to my role as IBM's first Chief Accessibility Officer.

The Human Ability and Accessibility Center was a global organization based in the prestigious IBM Research division. It was set up originally to leverage the best research talent to help address the increasing concerns of technology's impact on people with disabilities and people who are aging. Unlike other companies that viewed this concern through the lens of ADA (Americans with Disabilities Act) compliance, we took an innovation view from the very start. Our mission was to think beyond compliance and create an inclusive environment for employees and inclusive products for customers with different needs and abilities—all in the name of enabling people to reach their highest potential in their work and in their lives.

What began as another executive leadership career position became so much more. In this role, I would combine a lifetime of my own experience being different with my technology background to inform my work. Like my first systems engineer position, I didn't have a background in the topic, but as a result, I wasn't aware of the prevailing perceptions about accessibility. Rather than viewing it as compliance or charity, I was able to see the facts, from a business angle, and I was amazed by my team. They were incredibly creative, out-of-the-box thinkers, and their brilliant approach was often fueled—rather than limited—by their disabilities. This was the power of difference at play.

The potential of this work became increasingly clear to me: Because growth and innovation were happening so rapidly, we had the opportunity to change people's lives for the better through better tech. I also understood what we had to gain: productivity, insight, and ideas from intelligent, talented people whose ability to contribute had been hindered by limitations in technology and in the perspective of those around them. And so, what started as a job quickly transformed into a calling. I would also have the opportunity to follow in my father's footsteps and do my own UN work. I spoke at the UN and testified in front of the US Senate in support of the ratification of the UN Convention on the Rights of Persons with Disabilities, an international disability treaty modeled on the Americans with Disabilities Act. It was truly one of my greatest professional accomplishments.

In 2016, I decided to go out on my own, to follow my calling down a path that broadens the reach of Authentic Inclusion—not within a single company, but throughout the business world. The goal of my speaking engagements and strategy advisory work now is to awaken decision-makers at institutions—from the founders of quickly growing startups to the CEOs of established giants in the field and government officials around the world—to the potential of Authentic Inclusion. I want them to understand how much profit, innovation, employee and customer loyalty, citizen happiness, and positive cultural change they can create with some philosophical and organizational changes at their organizations.

To see how this plays out, let's see what happens when companies embody the tenets of Authentic Inclusion from the start—and what happens when they don't.

CHAPTER 3
Humans Putting Humans First: Technology by People, for People

Many of the world's societies have gone through multiple stages of evolution. They have transformed from communities of hunter-gatherers to horticultural and pastoral cultures—growing crops and raising livestock with simple tools—to agricultural ones, where more complex tools and devices helped increase production. Then, they became industrialized, fueled by factories, machines, and automation. Now, in postindustrial societies, information and technology dominate, and technology—and its purpose—continues to evolve. Much like the stages of society, technology's role started out simple and is becoming increasingly more complex. As technology moves from the back office to our front pockets, becoming involved in every aspect of our lives, we need to be all the more aware—and deliberate—about the human-like functions we build in.

THE ERA OF THE MAINFRAME

The purpose of the early generation of computers was to help businesses to process large amounts of information efficiently. As such, designers focused primarily on processing speed and handling a high volume of input and output. It was not about personal use. Back in 1979, when I first joined IBM, it was the era of the mainframe. At that time, nobody had their own computer. If you wanted to use one, you'd have to go to the computer center at a university or a service bureau. You'd put your program on punch cards and take them to a data center where someone would enter them for you. You would then wait to collect your printout on a big sheet of paper with green bars running across it (we called it "watermelon paper"). It required a lot of attention and advance planning, and there was nothing user-friendly about it.

I was working on accounts for large manufacturing companies and banks. As a systems engineer, my job was to figure out the level of computing power my customers would need to manage their shop floor systems or speed up their check-processing systems. I was very enthusiastic about helping my customers install these so-called "enterprise mainframe systems" to address their business challenges. My inspiration at the time was to follow the prior generation of IBMers who had engaged in projects that "had a higher calling," as one of my mentors said. For example, IBM assisted with the development of computer systems for NASA's Project Apollo and created solutions for the Social Security Administration. Their work and focus were not just about a system's power or speed; they were about solving difficult problems impacting humanity—a quality that always made me very proud to be an IBMer. Still, the technology at the time was designed to solve a "system" problem, not an "individual" problem.

THE RISE OF THE PC

It wasn't until the 1980s that the tech economy shifted from a system to a personal focus. In August of 1981, IBM released the transformative IBM PC, finally providing small businesses and individuals with the power of independent computing. The first generation of personal computers had made their way into the world, but in actuality, they weren't very personal; they were primarily used by those with specialized training in the technology or by individuals in the business world.

At first, the applications they offered regular people were pretty basic—and they were still all about speed and process automation. I remember lugging home a very early version of the PC to help my husband type up his dissertation, the sole purpose being to make word processing more efficient than it would have been on a typewriter.

Then, in the late 1980s and early 1990s, Microsoft and Apple began to grow, and the PC market blossomed. That period was a profound time for the tech industry, for the economy, and for me personally. With the rise of the PC in the early 1990s, and the growth of the internet and Silicon Valley later that decade, the focus began to shift. Technology became democratized and consumerized. Rather than serving business systems, it began serving individual people. From games to mobile phones and social media, tech was soon woven into the fabric of our existence. Today, it underpins almost everything we do—how we work, play, and live. It's about so much more than productivity; for many of us, our data has become our lives. Our digital presence, in some cases, defines who we are.

Moreover, in addition to improving systems—be it in manufacturing, banking, retail, or even word processing—much of today's technology is focused on improving people. Through technology, we have been able to personalize the tools we use to help us become the best version of ourselves. Apps, websites, and online services offer us health care, education, banking, and so much more—all tailored to our schedules, needs, and interests. That level of functionality is powered by smarter technology that makes human considerations and decisions for us in exchange for convenience, productivity, and customization. We are becoming a society where technology and people are increasingly intertwined.

THE IMPORTANCE—AND RESPONSIBILITY— OF ACCESSIBILITY

The technology we are creating today will likely be a partner in everything we do. This seismic shift necessitates a corresponding metamorphosis in our mindset: since technology is becoming ever more personal, the diversity of humanity and human thinking should be added into the stack.

Customer-centricity is about extreme personalization, and accessibility is part of that: ensuring that everyone who uses your product or service, regardless of their age or ability, is able to have the same positive—or even delightful—experience. It is no longer feasible to build a system and expect to go back and adapt it later for, say, a blind user. To slow down and retrofit technology after the fact essentially means that you are doing the job twice, costing you time and money and putting you at a competitive disadvantage. Precisely because of the rapid growth we are experiencing, it really does benefit us to be as mindful and intentional as possible.

In addition, because of the speed at which technology moves, if the technologists of today—the ones programming the tools that have become so pervasive in our lives—represent limited backgrounds, experiences, and perspectives, we risk unconsciously embedding those biases into everything we do.

Artificial intelligence is a good example of a technology that suffers when there is limited input. Imagine, for example, that a series of care robots developed to tend to the elderly were designed exclusively by twenty-five-year-old white men—which is not unlikely, considering that, in 2016, around 80 percent of US computer science graduates were male and 63 percent were white—a statistic that indicates the need for diversity much earlier in the pipeline.[3]

It's easy to imagine the myriad ways in which technology for the elderly built and tested exclusively by twenty-five-year-olds might fall short, not just because that cohort of developers is less likely to have significant firsthand experience with the needs of the demographic but also because the limited perspective of a homogenous group is bound to miss both design issues and opportunities. Would the care robot take into account your grandmother's feminine issues or her weakened vision and knees? Would it be able to gauge her loneliness based on the tonality of her response?

With AI, it's not just about speed or function; we're talking about designing more intangible human qualities. It's about emotion, connection, interaction. That kind of logic and nuance has to be built into the new artificial intelligence, and doing that effectively requires that you include diverse design partners in your process—people of different ages, genders, cultures, and physical abilities, to name a few. If you do, whatever it is you are building is much more likely to serve its purpose in a broad and enduring way, because you will have considered a range of human use, rather than just one perspective.

THE PITFALLS OF LIMITED INCLUSION

We've all experienced the pitfalls of limited perspective in one way or another—encountering a product, service, or event that didn't take into account or address our unique needs. One particular occasion early in my career served as an eye-opening experience in this regard,

---

3   Bianca Myers, "Women and Minorities in Tech, by the Numbers," *Wired*, March 27, 2018, https://www.wired.com/story/computer-science-graduates-diversity/.

to say the least. I had been named Systems Engineer "Rookie of the Year" and was invited to attend a prestigious IBM systems engineering recognition event at the Fontainebleau Hotel in Miami Beach. As a reward, those of us being recognized could choose from free activities such as golf, tennis, or deep-sea fishing. Since I'd never played golf or tennis, fishing seemed like the safest choice.

As it turned out, the reality of the day was quite different from what I had imagined. I endured six hours at sea with half a dozen beer-drinking men. There was no shade anywhere, and no one for me to talk to. Since I didn't drink, I stood with the captain, feeling my skin burn in the Florida sun, while everyone else drank beer, told jokes, and talked about fishing. Those were the six longest hours of my life. When I got back to dry land, I realized that the event had felt much more like a punishment than a reward.

I remember thinking to myself that the event planners probably spent a lot of time and money in coming up with activity options. But they clearly had one type of employee in mind—and that person did not resemble me. As a result, it was difficult, if not impossible, for me to feel welcome in that situation.

We see this in tech all the time. Have you ever been on a website where the content scrolls too quickly for you grasp its meaning? While the design experience may work for a twenty-something native English speaker who can read very quickly, for many others it might be quite hard to catch. The issue extends beyond ability. Perhaps you've tried to look up a restaurant's menu on your phone, only to realize that the site isn't optimized for mobile. Considering whether the website's readers will be able to digest the information in time, whether the format is ideal, and whether you're achieving your desired outcome are all important aspects of the design process that benefit from a diversity of insights and experiences.

More than just causing frustration for users, a lack of accessibility can have serious consequences in the form of lawsuits and other penalties. In 2006, a blind University of California, Berkeley student, Bruce Sexton, found that he was unable to shop on Target's website due to its inaccessibility. Without "alt text," or descriptions of images used by screen-reading technology, and accessible image maps embedded in the website, it was impossible for blind people to complete a purchase at target.com on their own.[4] Together with the National Federation of the Blind (NFB), he filed a class-action suit citing violations of civil rights, the Americans with Disabilities Act (ADA), and a number of California statutes. Target eventually settled with the NFB, paying $6 million to members of the suit, in addition to the significant costs of updating its site to be accessible.[5]

THE BENEFITS OF INCLUSION FAR EXCEED COMPLIANCE

As Sexton posited in the Target case, increasing accessibility would not only "reach 1.3 million people in this nation and the growing baby boomer population who will also be losing vision," but also improve navigability overall, and this holds true for other aspects of tech as well.[6] Increasing accessibility benefits all of us, adding a layer of functionality and personalization that serves users in myriad circumstances.

Take the increasing prevalence of video on the Internet. As the web progressed from a text-based format and video became a common aspect of our online experience, designers and programmers had to evolve to make the format accessible, introducing captioning. Captioning doesn't just benefit those using screen readers or those who are

---

4 Henry Lee, "Blind Cal Student Sues Target/Suit Charges Retailer's Web Site Cannot Be Used by the Sightless," *SF Gate*, February 8, 2006, https://www.sfgate.com/news/article/Blind-Cal-student-sues-Target-Suit-charges-2504938.php.

5 David Chartier, "Target to Pay $6 Million to Settle Site Accessibility Suit," *Ars Technica*, August 28, 2018, https://arstechnica.com/uncategorized/2008/08/target-to-pay-6-million-to-settle-site-accessibility-suit/.

6 Lee, "Blind Cal Student Sues Target."

deaf. The inclusion of text allows all users to access the information efficiently, including people who cannot understand spoken English but can read it or who are experiencing limited ability based on their surroundings, such as in areas with ambient noise, like the airport.

Companies are catching on to the significant benefits accessibility brings, too, offering consumers numerous ways to get the information they need. Even in countries where disability laws like the ADA don't play a role in product and service development, such as China, businesses are focusing on this area as a manner of differentiating themselves and finding financial success. For example, after learning about the impact of their inaccessible mobile platform, one of China's largest fintech companies hired diverse design and testing teams—comprising people of all ages and abilities—to ensure the user experience was embedded into every step of the company's processes. And as a result, they have been able to build a better product and reach previously untapped markets.

The European-based company Inclusite, a human-centric technology solutions company focused on making IT infrastructure usable by all, is also investing in accessibility as a business imperative and a route to serve new markets.[7] In 2017, the company was awarded the World Emerging Digital Award by the World Information Technology and Services Alliance (WITSA), an organization representing 90 percent of ICT companies around the globe, at the 2017 World Congress on IT. The congress was held in my hometown, Taipei, Taiwan, and it was very rewarding to see a company doing excellent work to move the needle on digital inclusion recognized in the place where my own inclusion journey began.[8]

A recent winner of MassChallenge, a startup accelerator and

---

7   "About Us," Inclusite, accessed November 13, 2018, https://www.inclusite.com/about-us/.

8   "About Us," Inclusite.

competition that supports high-impact, early-stage entrepreneurs, also demonstrated the value of the extreme personalization offered by accessibility. Medumo, a service available to health-care providers and their patients, provides timely automated instructions and check-lists to support patients before, during, and after various medical procedures. The various CareTours offered by the program enable personalization while minimizing administrative time. Customized instructions are delivered via text or voice—allowing almost anyone to access the health information they need when they need it.

These are just a few examples of what the present and future of human-centered—or human-first—tech looks like. In a world where personalization is at the heart of tech, including diversity and adhering to the tenets of accessibility at every step of the way are both protective and profitable measures. But we also owe it to the world to deliver on the fundamental promises of technology: equalizing access, creating democracy, and fulfilling our human potential. That's the opportunity in front of us.

Doing so requires that all companies—from startups to tech giants—find people who represent perspectives that may not yet be in the room. These are the people who represent your broadest customer base. They are the ones who are going to help drive lasting, human-first innovation. And creating a workplace that cultivates their input is the enrichment factor, the secret sauce that will make our technol-ogy—and our world—that much better. To understand how to build an environment that enables all of us to be our best, let's first consider local and global business psychology.

CHAPTER 4
Shifting Business Perspectives for Disruptive Innovation: From Fortune 500 to Impact 500

While the world is changing more rapidly than ever, it's not uncommon to get stuck in old thought patterns—particularly if our policies, practices, and personnel lack the diversity that is necessary to anticipate the change and to drive disruptive innovation. In a global, interconnected marketplace, however, there is immense potential to change our thinking and create both progress and profit. In this chapter, we will flip the script on conventional business wisdom, explore the potential for America to be a leader in accessibility, digital inclusion, and beyond, and discuss a crucial aspect of our strategy: where to begin.

Let's start with some common perceptions in our business culture, and the shifts in perspective that have the power to transform our behavior and our impact.

INTELLECT VS. INSTINCT

We know extreme personalization is becoming the primary differentiator in business success. Michael Schrage, a research fellow at the Massachusetts Institute of Technology's Center for Digital Business and an expert on innovation, highlights this reality in his book, *The Innovator's Hypothesis: How Cheap Experiments Are Worth More Than Good Ideas*. He asserts that "successful innovators have a 'vision of the customer future' that matters every bit as much as their product or service vision. By treating innovation as an investment in customer futures, organizations can make their customers more valuable. In other words, 'Making Customers Better Makes Better Customers.'"[9]

This is especially powerful when we consider that people with disabilities—1.3 billion individuals around the globe—represent $8 trillion in disposable income.[10] Creating accessible technology and solutions that help *all* customers and clients become the best versions of themselves can open up untapped markets and significantly benefit bottom lines.

To compete in today's business world, we have to do this as quickly as possible, evolving along with customer and client needs. But this rationale is sometimes at odds with the typical business mindset, which tends to favor thinking and planning over instinct and action. We often get bogged down in rounds of meetings, levels of resistance, and concerns about the cost of implementing something new.

So, what's the solution? Schrage found that it was experimentation. He discovered that experimentation "didn't just offer the best way to cost-effectively invest in innovation; it offered the most inno-

---

9   Michael Schrage, *The Innovator's Hypothesis: How Cheap Experiments Are Worth More Than Good Ideas*, Boston: Massachusetts Institute of Technology, 2014.
10   Robert Reiss, "Business's Next Frontier: People with Disabilities," *Forbes*, July 30, 2014, https://www.forbes.com/sites/robertreiss/2015/07/30/businesss-next-frontier-people-with-disabilities/#2c09a0b4104a.

vative way of exploring how to invest in the human capital, competences, and capabilities of one's customers."[11]

Imposing time and cost limits on experimentation also fuels powerful ideas and actions. There is a Chinese adage that echoes this sentiment: "If you are poor, you will try to change. If you are really, really poor, you will start to transform." I used this saying at IBM all the time, as we worked to do more with less—driving impactful results with fewer resources.

By the same token, when life's circumstances are not accommodating—as is the case for many people who differ from the majority—we must adapt to surroundings that aren't built to serve our needs. This makes us resourceful and innovative and puts us in tune with others who face similar roadblocks. That's why Authentic Inclusion—bringing people on board who have a variety of experiences, abilities, and perspectives—can be a primary source of disruptive innovation.

PROFIT VS. PURPOSE

Creating true innovation in technology and business doesn't necessarily require a lot of money, but it does demand an investment in humanity. Rather than just focus on profits—as many businesses tend to do—we have to consider the broad range of human interests, preferences, behavior, and interactions to figure out the best next move.

Steve Jobs understood the value of human wants, and he used that understanding to crack the code of simplicity with Apple, capitalizing on people's desire for intuitive products that folded seamlessly into their lives. He followed his instincts and his understanding of human interactions and married those insights with technology for a purpose-driven approach that prioritizes the customer.

Peter Hartigan, a Stanford MBA and venture capitalist, envisions

---

11   Schrage, *The Innovator's Hypothesis.*

a future in which businesses take Apple's purposeful approach to the next level. He began thinking beyond the Fortune 500, which is dictated entirely by revenue and profit, to come up with a different set of criteria—one that would measure societal impact alongside company earnings. He arrived at something he calls the Impact500, "where community, transparency, and accountability are core competitive advantages."[12] The companies that make this list are dedicated to improving their communities, and as a result, they are more profitable than many of their profit-focused peers. The thesis behind the Impact500 is that seeking out human value and impact adds to, rather than limits, economic value.

SHORT TERM VS. LONG TERM

Accomplishing any real change also requires us to implement a different timeline—one that may be longer than what we are used to. Businesses often evaluate success in the short term, but many CEOs are beginning to realize that patience pays off. For example, in August 2018, Elon Musk, one of the most recognized innovators of our time, threatened via tweet to take Tesla private, citing the stock market's tendency to be shortsighted in its obsession with short-term outcomes.[13]

In an e-mail sent to Tesla employees after his social media announcement, Musk explained that swings in stock price and a focus on quarterly earnings "[put] enormous pressure on Tesla to make decisions that may be right for a given quarter, but not necessarily right for the long term," stating, "I fundamentally believe that we are at our best when everyone is focused on executing, when we can remain focused on our long-term mission, and when there are

---

12 "Innovating a Human Future of Work," *Encyclopedia*, Accessed September 19, 2018, http://i4j.info/encyclopedia/pete-hartigan/.

13 Neal E. Boudette and Matt Phillips, "Elon Musk Says Tesla May Go Private, and Its Stock Soars," *New York Times*, August 7, 2018, https://www.nytimes.com/2018/08/07/business/tesla-stock-elon-musk-private.html.

not perverse incentives for people to try to harm what we're all trying to achieve."[14]

While Musk's tweet sent his stock soaring and launched a firestorm of speculation about whether he could actually take Tesla private, his concern raises an important point about the benefits of long-term thinking. Maximizing everything for short-term profits often means sacrificing long-term gain.

It can take years to see the negative effects of short-term choices, especially with technology that is responsive down to the nanosecond. At the push of a button, Google comes back with ten million search results, and yet the long-term impact of this innovation on humanity is much harder to predict. For example, as social media has evolved—becoming more and more a part of our everyday lives—so have a multitude of unanticipated societal challenges like cyberbullying and fake news. Tremendous attention must be paid to what exactly we are designing and its potential impact on all of us today, tomorrow, and many years down the line.

FEEDING VS. FEELING

We must also consider the way we conceptualize our goals and the policies and practices that can get us there. Groupthink afflicts much of American society. There's a wave of pressure to conform to the program de jour, whether it's fashion, diet, exercise, or business principles. When I was pregnant with my first child, rather than head down the rabbit hole of resources on pregnancy and childbirth, I chose to feel it out, listening to my body over the thousands of experts out there. But my friends and colleagues didn't approve of the fact that I wasn't reading all the right books on pregnancy and

---

14   Elon Musk, "Taking Tesla Private," Tesla, August 7, 2018, https://www.tesla.com/blog/taking-tesla-private?redirect=no.

childbirth, and they didn't hold back when it came to sharing their disappointment.

You can easily feel like an outcast if you don't read the "right" books and come to the "right" conclusions. We are fed prescriptions on the "right" way to do business all the time, rarely taking into account the differences of individual circumstances or the needs of individual customers. But since the future of business and technology is much more personal than its past, we have to move away from the rigidity of common business conceptions, which often limit access for those who aren't part of the majority. Feeling it out by combining human wants and interests with business priorities—instead of the prescriptions for success that we are often fed—promotes inclusion and profit longevity. For instance, what if the VCs who control billions of dollars in investment funding made digital inclusion part of their funding criteria? This small shift could change the landscape of business and accessibility at large—and create new channels for revenue from an underserved market in the process.

Feeling things out also helps us avoid some of the significant downsides of groupthink. In the previous chapter, we discussed some of the ways a homogenous demographic of programmers and designers affects the technology we create, one of them being that we can embed our own limited perspective into technology. That limited perspective can also affect bottom lines. For example, on February 5, 2018, the Dow Jones Industrial Average experienced its worst-ever decline in a single day. The drop may have been due to automated sell-stop orders, which prevent losses by triggering a sale when a stock price begins to drop. In this case, there were many, many machines acting like the humans that programmed them—all at the same time. Experts believe that the prevalence of automated strategies like this one may make the market more prone to wild swings in the future, an unintended consequence that could hurt investors' profits.[15]

In addition, when our biases—conscious or unconscious—are woven into the fabric of technology, we can create a much bigger problem: inadvertently promoting a culture of discrimination and inequality. Automated decision-making systems are used for a number of functions, from determining credit scores to predicting whether people who are convicted of crimes will reoffend. We rely on these tools to remove some of the human biases that show up in our interactions with one another, but if we don't consider the impact of the people behind the programs, we may end up doing exactly the opposite.

For instance, a 2015 *Consumer Reports* investigation found that car insurance companies' automated systems were awarding the lowest insurance quotes to those with high credit scores, rather than to good drivers. Those with perfect driving records and low credit scores paid around $1,552 more than those with good credit who had been convicted of driving drunk.[16] Programmers had built their own preconceived notions into the system itself, and the system was acting accordingly.

The more these automated loops are reinforced, the harder they are to undo, and the more damage they can create. In this case, the human biases in our technology have the potential to contribute to poverty, raising insurance prices for low-income individuals and creating a cycle of high debt and low credit scores that can affect every aspect of their lives.[17]

Companies are addressing these issues, teaching machines to

---

15 Stephanie Yang, "When Machines (and Humans) Decide to Sell at Once," *Wall Street Journal*, September 3, 2018, https://www.wsj.com/articles/when-machines-and-humans-decide-to-sell-at-once-1535976000.

16 Cristina Couch, "Ghosts in the Machine," *Nova Next*, October 25, 2017, http://www.pbs.org/wgbh/nova/next/tech/ai-bias/.

17 Couch, "Ghosts in the Machine."

look at a variety of factors to bring about more fair and equitable treatment. IBM's AI Fairness 360—"a comprehensive open-source toolkit of metrics to check for unwanted bias in datasets and machine learning models, and state-of-the-art algorithms to mitigate such bias"—is one such example.[18] Cultivating fair and equitable consciousness from the beginning—rather than course correcting once things have gone too far south—will save time and money in the end. Doing so will require some decision making and investments. Fortunately, the United States has the legislative foundation to support such a shift.

INCREASING ACCESSIBILITY: A GLOBAL (AND PERSONAL) PRIORITY

The US set the standard for accessibility in 1990 with the Americans with Disabilities Act (ADA). Prohibiting discrimination against people with disabilities and aiming to ensure equal access to employment, transportation, accommodations, communications, and government programs and services, the ADA was signed into law on July 26, 1990, by George H.W. Bush, who counted it among his biggest accomplishments while in office.[19], [20]

The law was inspiring on the world stage, influencing the United Nations' Convention on the Rights of Persons with Disabilities (CRPD), the first convention of its kind in the twenty-first century. The CRPD transformed disability from a civil rights issue into a human rights issue, "[taking] to a new height the movement

---

18 "Introducing AI Fairness 360," IBM, September 19, 2018. https://www.ibm.com/blogs/research/2018/09/ai-fairness-360/.

19 "Americans with Disabilities Act," US Department of Labor, accessed September 19, 2018, https://www.dol.gov/general/topic/disability/ada.

20 "George H.W. Bush: 41st President of the United States," Academy of Achievement, accessed September 19, 2018, http://www.achievement.org/achiever/george-h-w-bush/.

from viewing persons with disabilities as 'objects' of charity, medical treatment, and social protection towards viewing persons with disabilities as 'subjects' with rights, who are capable of claiming those rights and making decisions for their lives."[21] The convention was negotiated over the course of eight sessions held from 2002 to 2006, making it the fastest-negotiated human rights treaty in history.[22] It was also the first time a human rights treaty discussed the importance of technology in leveling the playing field—a discussion captured in Article 9 of the convention.

I helped with the development of the CRPD through my engagement with G3ict, the Global Initiative for Inclusive Information and Communication Technologies, a nonprofit focused on promoting the rights of people with disabilities in the digital age. G3ict president and founder Axel Leblois, a highly successful French business executive; Ambassador Luis Gallegos, chair of the board of trustees of G3ict and Permanent Representative of Ecuador to the United Nations at the time; and I met in the lobby of the Millennium Hotel—right next to the UN—in 2006 for the organization's very first meeting.[23] The three of us had different nationalities and different professional paths, but we shared one goal: to do something meaningful to advance the digital rights of people with disabilities around the world.

Ambassador Gallegos served as a key sponsor in putting forward the CRPD, and I spoke in support of it—delivering a keynote at the UN in 2006 that emphasized how expanding human rights is good

21   "Convention on the Rights of Persons with Disabilities (CRPD)," United Nations, accessed September 19, 2018, https://www.un.org/development/desa/disabilities/convention-on-the-rights-of-persons-with-disabilities.html.
22   "Convention on the Rights of Persons with Disabilities."
23   G3ict, "Frances West, Global Thought Leader in Digital Accessibility, to Chair G3ict Strategy and Development Committee," press release, July 7, 2016, http://g3ict.org/news-releases/frances-west-global-thought-leader-in-digital-accessibility-to-chair-g3ict-strategy-and-development-committee.

for business. As I walked through the doors of the UN that day, I thought of my father's own UN work. My mother had been right: I was more like him than my brothers were, and I was grateful for the access and opportunity that had allowed me to carry on his legacy.

The CRPD was opened for signature in March of 2007. As of 2018, 177 countries have ratified it and are using it to inform their policies. And because the treaty itself discusses the necessity of accessible technology in an equitable society, that is part of the commitment the participating countries made when signing on.

Those of us who were involved in the convention wanted the US to be one of the major participants, to continue to set the standard for the rest of the world. However, while the Obama Administration signed the treaty in 2009 and affirmed their belief in its value, the US Senate failed to ratify it, making the US one of only a handful of countries that hasn't formally approved it, along with Libya, Bhutan, Uzbekistan, and Kyrgyzstan.[24]

Despite the fact that the US has not ratified the CRPD, we still have the history and groundwork to make progress. Our own legislation—including the ADA and Section 508, a provision of the Rehabilitation Act of 1973 that "[mandates] that all electronic and information technology developed, procured, maintained or used by the federal government be accessible to people with disabilities"— emphasizes the necessity of accessibility and inclusion. While Section 508 doesn't apply to the private sector, it dictates that any company or organization that does business with the federal government must comply with its guidelines, with fully accessible technology.[25] To be considered "accessible," technology must be as usable to people with

---

24 G3ict, "Frances West, Global Thought Leader."
25 Margaret Rouse, "Section 508," TechTarget, accessed November 1, 2018. https://searchcio.techtarget.com/definition/Section-508.

disabilities as it is to those without them. [26]

States are also beginning to pass similar accessibility legislation, with California, New York, Massachusetts, and Texas leading the way. In addition, thanks to social media, people are gaining a better understanding of the Americans with Disabilities Act and the rights it affords them. With a strong baseline in place, we can—and should—continue raising the bar on accessibility, but we will have to work to keep up with other countries' advances.

A PROACTIVE APPROACH—WITH TECHNOLOGY TO MATCH

Some countries are taking a base-level approach to this growing issue, aiming to craft legislation and policies that ensure compliance. Canada just presented its first accessibility law, the Accessible Canada Act, with the goal of removing barriers to accessibility, defined as "anything 'architectural, physical, technological, or attitudinal' that 'hinders the full participation in society of a physical, mental, intellectual, learning, communication, or sensory impairment.'"[27]

While removing barriers is a good start, others are beginning to take a much more proactive and innovation-based approach. Australia is engaged in a social experiment called the National Disability Insurance Scheme (NDIS), which aims to empower people with disabilities to determine the services they need.

Typically, a government sets aside funds for services for people with disabilities, which are then administrated by a third party—such as a state agency. But as part of this new program, the Australian government will deliver the funding directly to its citizens, recognizing that they have not only the right but also the capability, to make decisions about their own care.

---

26   Rouse, "Section 508."
27   Michelle McQuigge, "Canada's First National Accessibility Law Tabled in Ottawa," *The Canadian Press*, June 21, 2018.

To facilitate the country's switch to a new system and a new way of thinking, the Australian government is experimenting with new technology: a virtual assistant to help people navigate their options. Partnering with Academy Award-winner Mark Sagar—the AI engineer behind blockbuster movies like *Avatar* and *King Kong*—and people with disabilities, caregivers, advocacy groups, and other stakeholders, they created Nadia, a friendly virtual assistant. Nadia has a warm voice—provided by actress Cate Blanchett—to make her appealing to users, and technology from IBM Watson's team that enables her to listen, respond, and learn from each interaction.[28] With its extensive capabilities, Nadia could take many of the six thousand weekly calls that the NDIS's human representatives currently field, saving the Australian government more than $7.8 million annually.[29]

While the technology is still being developed and the project has faced some challenges, Australia's commitment to innovate—and improving its services, reach, and cost savings in the process—demonstrates the vast potential of integrating accessibility into business and technology from day one. A project like this one certainly involves risk, but there is also the potential for significant rewards.

BEGIN WITH THE ABCS

With an understanding of the many benefits of accessibility—legal, moral, cultural, innovative, and more—we need to think about closing the gap between acknowledging its value and putting into place the structures that make it possible. One way to do that is to prioritize accessibility at the entrance to the pipeline: education.

Universities are recognizing the downstream impact of their

---

28 Andrew Probyn, "NDIS' Virtual Assistant Nadia, Voiced by Cate Blanchett, Stalls After Recent Census, Robo-Debt Bungles," ABC, September 21, 2017, http://mobile.abc.net.au/news/2017-09-21/government-stalls-ndis-virtual-assistant-voiced-by-cate-blanchet/8968074.
29 Probyn, "NDIS' Virtual Assistant."

actions on society and modifying their practices accordingly. They understand that opening their doors to students from all segments of society will create an environment that allows more people to succeed. Princeton is transforming its financial aid program to make college accessible for students from a variety of socioeconomic backgrounds, and instituting holistic practices that are enabling 82 percent of students to graduate debt free.[30] The NYU School of Medicine recently announced that it would make tuition free for all current and future students, with the idea that lifting the tremendous financial burden of medical education will inspire doctors to pursue crucial but lesser-paying specialties, such as family medicine and pediatrics.[31] But along with providing academic access to a broader, more diverse pool of people, we also need to consider what we teach them.

When weighing the human impact of our business decisions, we can start with the humans who are most likely to occupy the executive suite: business school students.

Over the course of my professional career, as I took executive education courses at Harvard, Wharton, and other elite schools that produce many of today's business leaders, I began to understand that much of our conventional business thinking comes from these institutions. Many heads of Silicon Valley tech companies, venture capital firms, hedge funds, and global organizations attend the same top business schools, learning from thinkers and practitioners with similar backgrounds to their own. Because business schools play such a dominant role in shaping the mindset of our business leaders, we must educate the next generation of executives to think about the alignment of purpose and profit before they become our primary decision-makers.

---

30   "Affordable for All," Princeton University, accessed September 19, 2018, https://www.princeton.edu/admission-aid/affordable-all.

31   David W. Chen, "Surprise Gift: Free Tuition for All NYU Medical Students," *New York Times*, August 6, 2018.

Technology is also part of this equation, as it forms most business platforms. Accessibility and digital inclusion should be a required part of the core curriculum in computer- and data-science programs. Yet, very few universities offer courses on accessible design or programming. Instead, most user experience—or UX—courses only take into account people with typical abilities.

We should be striving for an accessible experience that is not only compliant but also usable: websites and programs that don't just work with accessibility tools, but that also display logically and provide ease of navigation for anyone using them, via any route. These are the kinds of tools that equalize work, play, and other crucial aspects of our day-to-day lives. As Michael Schrage says, helping our customers to be better will also make them better customers, and instilling this crucial concept in our collective consciousness begins in the classroom.

EVALUATING OUR APPROACH TO RESEARCH

Another way to ingrain the principles of accessibility into society is to address research: the processes that grow our understanding of the world. Much of our work focuses on the majority, but when we broaden our scope to include diverse populations, we can serve everyone better. Moreover, if we can use research to establish accessibility as a logical competitive advantage, we can convince leaders who are hesitant to embrace inclusive practices to expand their thinking.

With this in mind, I began talking with Dr. Jennifer Lerner, professor of public policy and management at Harvard Kennedy School of Government and cofounder of the Harvard Decision Science Laboratory. Knowing that so many of our business and tech policies and processes come from the top, we began to brainstorm what a human-first research scenario might look like. For instance, could we initiate a study with students at the Harvard Kennedy and Business Schools to explore executives' thinking and determine if and how behavioral science can transform their understanding of inclusive employment—and help them take action to cultivate it in their organizations? This kind of research, which combines human thinking and decision-science technology, has the potential to shape both business and society, influencing government policies and launching innovative strategies that will help integrate purpose and profit.

We've covered some of the challenges our current environment poses to diversity and inclusion, such as the prevailing business mindset in the US. But we've also looked at many of the big opportunities we have to usher in inclusive change—the laws promoting inclusion that are already in place, the chance to embed inclusive thinking in the curricula of top business schools and data- and computer-science programs, and the vast potential of taking a human-first approach to decision science and behavioral research. Now, we need to focus on getting the diverse voices necessary to make these meaningful changes involved in the process.

CHAPTER 5

Integrating Humans Back into the Talent and Technology Process: Don't Let AI Reject Your Best Candidates

I so clearly remember that first IBM interview back in 1979 in Lexington, Kentucky. It was April—a beautiful day. My appointment was early in the week, and I spent the whole weekend prior practicing the interviewer's name: *Friedersdorf, Friedersdorf, Friedersdorf*—three complex syllables that felt so foreign to me. I wanted to be polite. I wanted to say, "Hi Mr. Friedersdorf, nice to meet you" as flawlessly as possible. My husband and I worked on my handshake too, as I tried to get the right grip—one that would convey a level of capability that my words might fail to capture.

When we finally met, Frank Friedersdorf—a white, German man—sat before me, a Chinese woman still working to grasp the English language. I was nervous, but sitting down face to face, I could sense the rhythm of the conversation. When I hesitated or searched for the right English word, I could tell that Mr. Frieder-sdorf was not impatient with me. Instead, he was engaged by our conversation, and that boosted my confidence. That human-to-human connection and feedback allowed me to perform to the best of my ability and land a position at the company where I would spend the majority of my career.

A CENTURY-LONG COMMITMENT TO DIVERSITY AND ACCESSIBILITY

Though I didn't know it at the time, my interview with Mr. Frie-dersdorf—and his willingness to give me a chance—reflected IBM's longstanding commitment to diversity and accessibility. IBM hired its first African-American employee in 1899 and its first employee with a disability in 1914, decades before the Civil Rights Act of 1964 and the Americans with Disabilities Act of 1990. It promoted its first female vice president in 1943, and in 1953, IBM became the first US corporation to mandate that employees would be hired without regard to race, color, or creed—a nondiscrimination policy that has since been expanded to encompass "religion, sex, gender, gender identity or expression, sexual orientation, national origin, genetics, disability, and age."[32]

IBM has worked to set the standard for accessible technology, inventing the first Braille printer, talking typewriter, and talking display terminal, and obtaining more than five hundred US patents for accessible technology over the years.[33] But beyond its techno-logical advancements, one of IBM's biggest accomplishments—and frankly, a vital element of competitive differentiation—was that it

32 "IBM: A Culture of Diversity and Inclusion," YouTube video, 2:27, September 20, 2017, https://www.youtube.com/watch?v=KRZi-Gy7u7E&app=desktop.
33 "The Accessible Workforce," IBM, accessed November 5, 2018. http://www03.ibm.com/ibm/history/ibm100/us/en/icons/accessibleworkforce/breakthroughs/

"operationalized" inclusion through accessibility.

What do I mean by "operationalized?" I mean taking an innovative and holistic approach to address accessibility at the enterprise or institutional level. While IBM is certainly creating usable assistive technology solutions for individuals—one of the latest examples being NavCog, a navigational cognitive assistant for the blind that uses AI Cloud technology, developed in collaboration with Carnegie Mellon's Cognitive Assistance Laboratory—it is just as focused on accessibility systems and tools that support the entire company.[34]

For example, IBM is a federal contractor, and one of the federal contract requirements under Section 508 is that each company needs to declare its product's accessibility status during the procurement proposal process through the Voluntary Product Accessibility Template, or VPAT. The VPAT is a self-reported form on which the vendor describes the ways the product meets Section 508 requirements.[35] To simplify this process, we created a checklist system to keep track of thousands of IBM products and their compliance. Because the system is automated, it can be modified to include other countries' standards, such as European Union procurement standard EN 301 549.[36]

Other examples include IBM's automated accessibility and content checkers. These tools were developed to help programmers check the accessibility of their work while they are developing new software, solutions, or apps. This is very important because as the DevOps cycle becomes shorter and shorter, the testing and validation of accessibility

---

34 "NavCog," Cognitive Assistance Lab, accessed November 1, 2018. http://www.cs.cmu.edu/~NavCog/navcog.html.

35 "Voluntary Product Accessibility Template," NC State University: IT Accessibility, accessed November 2, 2018. https://accessibility.oit.ncsu.edu/it-accessibility-at-nc-state/developers/accessibility-handbook/overview-understanding-the-nature-of-what-is-required-to-design-accessibly/voluntary-product-accessibility-template-vpat/.

36 "IBM Accessibility Checklist: Version 7.0," IBM, accessed November 1, 2018. https://www.ibm.com/able/guidelines/ci162/accessibility_checklist.html.

after development is completed becomes harder and harder.

Left unattended, many programmers would skip accessibility testing altogether. But with automated tools at their fingertips during the development cycle, making sure the code and the digital content are accessible becomes an easy and intuitive part of the process. Above all, systems like these ensure that individual designers and developers are upholding one of the IBM Accessibility organization's primary foci: leveraging technology innovations to help level the playing field and provide all people with the resources they need to reach their highest potential.

Since accessibility affects all people, this work is what I call "societal technology innovation," and it's a journey we should all be on together. Thus, IBM and other individuals and companies doing this work have to proactively engage other organizations to share our knowledge so that we can all help move the dial.

One specific action people and organizations can take is in the area of standards. IBM has always been a leader in the development of global accessibility standards that drive the creation of universally usable technology. It sponsors and collaborates with the World Wide Web Consortium (W3C) Web Accessibility Initiative, which sets guidelines for accessibility technology standards around the world and contributes to a more accessible future with educational materials and research on the topic.[37]

This commitment to accessibility and its power to change lives are summed up in a 1952 letter Helen Keller wrote to IBM founder Thomas Watson. She wrote, "I wish to express gratitude to you, Mr. Watson, for the enlightened citizenship with which you encourage your engineers to devise mechanical and electrical aids for the blind in pursuing their varied occupations. The more openings you make

---

37   W3C, "About W3C WAI," accessed October 3, 2018, https://www.w3.org/WAI/about/.

for them in the wall of darkness through innovation, the greater will their contribution be to public service, both as productive workers and responsible members of society."[38]

INVESTING IN HUMAN POTENTIAL

Watson saw the potential of so many people that society often overlooks. He upheld the tenets of Authentic Inclusion, believing that employing diverse people—and creating tools to help them succeed—would increase IBM's ability to be a leader in the market-place and set the company on the inclusive course it continues to follow today. This single factor, in my opinion, is what helps IBM maintain its place in one of the most competitive industries—technology—after 107 years in the business.

Current research demonstrates just how right he was, proving that diverse companies outpace their less diverse counterparts in a number of ways. McKinsey found that the most racially and ethnically diverse companies were 35 percent more likely to have higher financial returns than their less diverse counterparts and that those with the highest rates of gender diversity were 15 percent more likely to outperform their peers financially.

In addition, employees with disabilities—who span every background and experience—have been shown to "build a more authentic, loyal, and creative culture" and contribute to company success with unique perspectives and skill sets.[39] Research from Accenture and the American Association of People with Disabilities (AAPD) shows that individuals with disabilities also boost bottom lines. Their study found that companies invested in creating an inclusive environment

---

38   Letter from Helen Keller to Thomas Watson, October 16, 1952.
39   Robert Reiss, "Business's Next Frontier: People with Disabilities," *Forbes*, July 30, 2015, https://www.forbes.com/sites/robertreiss/2015/07/30/businesss-next-frontier-people-with-disabilities/#3234f1b6104a.

for people with disabilities had 28 percent higher revenues than their less inclusive peers and double the net income. They also achieved 30 percent higher profit margins and had better shareholder returns.[40]

There is the compliance piece to consider, too—legislation requires that we hire workers with disabilities. The US Equal Opportunity Commission's 2018 goal calls for 12 percent of all federal agencies and 7.5 percent of federal contractors to be composed of people with disabilities. It also sets a goal for 2 percent of federal employees to have intellectual and developmental disabilities. But leading companies are beginning to tap into other benefits of a diverse workforce like the ones mentioned above, which far exceed compliance.[41] PepsiCo, American Express, and many others are launching initiatives to bring more people with disabilities on board to improve their culture, ideas, and financial success. In 2013, Pepsi created Pepsi Achieving Change Together, an initiative to hire people with disabilities for a variety of roles across the company. Marty Bean, the company's senior vice president of field sales, echoed Thomas Watson's approach, stating that the company "[sees] this not as a way to hire people with disabilities, but hiring the right people for the job."[42]

Individual differences also come with the potential for unique and important contributions. For instance, those who are neurodivergent—possessing neurological differences such as dyslexia, attention deficit hyperactivity disorder, and autism—often have an extraordinary aptitude for highly valuable skills, such as math, memory, and pattern recognition. This is particularly pertinent to STEM fields,

---

40 Denise Brodey, "People with Disabilities Want Paychecks Not Pity: Here's How Businesses are Helping," *Forbes*, November 2, 2018, https://www.forbes.com/sites/denisebrodey/2018/11/02/people-with-disabilities-want-paychecks-not-pity-heres-how-businesses-are-helping/#53324236533c.

41 US Equal Employment Opportunity Commission, "EEOC Issues Regulations on the Federal Government's Obligation to Engage in Affirmative Action for People with Disabilities," news release, January 3, 2017, https://www1.eeoc.gov//eeoc/newsroom/release/1-3-17.cfm?renderforprint=1.

42 Reiss, "Business's Next Frontier."

which are currently experiencing skill shortages.[43]

In addition to the innovative ideas and valuable skills those with differences bring to the table, today's workers want a diverse and inclusive culture. Eighty percent of workers who responded to a 2017 Deloitte survey on diversity report that inclusion in the workplace matters to them, with 39 percent sharing that they would leave their current company for one with more inclusive values."[44] Companies are taking note of this reality too. Kevin Cox, American Express's chief human resource officer, stated, "ensuring that people with disabilities see themselves and their needs reflected in our products and the services we offer is important. It's important to our customers, as well as to our workforce."[45]

As we continue to grow our understanding of the many benefits a diverse workforce offers, we should also recognize that to harness the vast potential of people who think and act differently from the status quo, we need to make sure they can get through the door. To do so, we should consider our hiring processes, and any obstacles—whether they are imposed by humans or machines—that prevent us from employing the best person for the job.

THE UNINTENDED ROADBLOCKS OF OUR CURRENT HIRING PROCESSES

Hiring was originally handled entirely by humans. The face-to-face interactions that were once an essential part of the process helped us identify candidates who might be able to offer something that couldn't

---

43   Robert Austin and Gary Pisano, "Neurodiversity as a Competitive Advantage," *Harvard Business Review*, May–June 2017, https://hbr.org/2017/05/neurodiversity-as-a-competitive-advantage.

44   Jane Foutty, Terri Cooper, and Shelly Zalis, "The Inclusion Imperative: Redefining Leadership," *Wall Street Journal*, September 4, 2018, https://deloitte.wsj.com/cio/2018/09/04/the-inclusion-imperative-redefining-leadership/https://deloitte.wsj.com/cio/2018/09/04/the-inclusion-imperative-redefining-leadership/.

45   Foutty, Cooper, and Zalis, "The Inclusion Imperative."

be captured in a résumé or cover letter. It was our human-to-human interaction that allowed Mr. Friedersdorf to see something in me.

Today, most job applications are online, and technology decides if and when candidates ever meet a human representative. Though technology and systemization make the hiring process more efficient and convenient, we have to think about the impact of turning over hiring decisions to machines, and what—and who—we lose when we don't consider exactly what we are programming those machines to do.

For one, if online job applications are not accessible to begin with, those with disabilities such as low vision or blindness—and much to offer our companies—may not even be able to apply. There are so many tools available to make sites usable for those with a variety of abilities. Employers make the choice to exclude those with disabilities when they do not incorporate accessibility features into their application sites—and in this day and age, there is little excuse for job application systems that don't work for everyone.

Unfortunately, even those who are able to clear the first hurdle by completing their application online may find themselves unable to reach the next level through no fault of their own. Online job applications are often advanced or eliminated based on keywords found in résumés and cover letters. But a lack of alignment between keywords identified by the employer and those provided by the applicant may indicate more about the employer's own identity and biases than an applicant's qualifications. For instance, words that are considered to be masculine, such as "lead," "compete," and "champion," often show up in job ads for male-dominated fields.[46] If the same keywords are used to select job applicants to move to the next stage, we risk inadvertently excluding highly qualified women from the pool of applicants.

---

46   Justin Friesen, Danielle Gaucher, and Aaron Kay, "Evidence That Gendered Wording in Job Advertisements Exists and Sustains Gender Inequality," *Journal of Personality and Social Psychology* 101, no. 1 (2011): 109–128.

Aging applicants often find themselves facing similar obstacles, with automated systems that can be set to eliminate applicants with many years of experience or ones that target candidates with keywords and language that focus on technological savvy.[47]

The few individuals who do make it through the online application screening may face yet another set of challenges when it comes time for the first human-driven part of the process: the in-person interview. People who communicate or interact in ways that differ from the norm—such as neurodiverse candidates—may find that the typical interview process does not do a great job of evaluating their skill set. As a result, the very differences that could offer employers tremendous efficiency and billion-dollar ideas may be dismissed in what HR departments and hiring managers deem a "lack of cultural fit."

To avoid eliminating top talent during the hiring process, we have to consider the systems we use—technology and otherwise—and determine whether they are truly serving the purpose we intend. If the answer is "no," it's time to pioneer different methods that more accurately evaluate skill and fit. For example, with the knowledge that people with autism could offer vital insight and contributions to the company, Microsoft launched its Autism Hiring Program in 2015. Rather than depending on the typical question-and-answer session that is often part of the interview process—which can pose challenges for people with autism—Microsoft created a multistep skills-assessment program to better observe candidates' technical and collaborative capabilities.[48] With this unique format, participants have numerous opportunities to demonstrate the many ways they

---

47   Jon Shields, "Age Discrimination: Older Applicants vs. 'Young Pretty People,'" Jobscan, March 5, 2018, https://www.jobscan.co/blog/age-discrimination-older-applicants-vs-young-pretty-people/.

48   Microsoft, "Inclusive Hiring for People with Disabilities," accessed September 28, 2018, https://www.microsoft.com/en-us/diversity/inside-microsoft/cross-disability/hiring.aspx.

can contribute to the organization.

Work Inc., a New England nonprofit with the mission "to ensure that all individuals with disabilities have the ability to grow, the right to make choices, access to education, and the opportunity to participate in community life via meaningful work," also uses a holistic assessment process to account for individuals' abilities. The organization runs a program called Pathways to Careers, an initiative that is open to anyone with significant disabilities. It determines employment matches by observing individual skills and interests.

The program's flexibility and personalization allow people with disabilities to find roles where they can be successful, even when their experiences don't seem to fit all the criteria. For example, one candidate did not have a high-school diploma—a requirement for the job he was interested in—but he had earned the rank of Eagle Scout from the Boy Scouts, an achievement that requires leadership, independence, teamwork, and tenacity. When the hiring manager learned of his accomplishment through Pathways to Careers' thorough process, she was able to recognize that he would be a good fit for the position, whereas an automated system may have eliminated him from the applicant pool based on his lack of diploma alone.

Fortunately, we have the capability to incorporate this very human approach to hiring into our technology. We can program our systems to "think" more broadly and recognize the value of nontraditional experience and skills. But we have to first use our humanity to increase the accessibility of our mindset and our processes.

And rather than focusing on one group at a time—building a system that works for a specific demographic and then reevaluating and reinventing the wheel as our awareness grows—we should address accessibility as a whole, creating multiple routes for hiring and accommodation from the beginning. Such an approach would save time and money and help ensure that we are not letting highly qualified candidates slip through the cracks with systems that can't accommodate them or recognize their talent.

INCLUSIVE HIRING GOES BEYOND HR

In an increasingly human-centric and technology-driven world, ingenuity and innovation start with people. To reflect your clients and customers and create the products and services they want and need, your talent pool has to be as diverse as possible. Most leaders understand this priority, at least on the surface: a recent Conference Board survey of executives around the world revealed that "talent and skills are now the number one hot-button issue for C-level executives, surpassing cybersecurity, healthcare, and threats to global trade."[49] But to effectively harness this talent, the systems we build must help—rather than hinder—us in cultivating a diverse workforce. It's just that simple.

Improving the technology behind our hiring and recruiting sites and processes is a good first step, but to truly embrace Authentic Inclusion, we have to go further. With the awareness that talent and skills play such a critical role in company success, it is only logical that leaders—CEOs, CIOs, CTOs, and other C-suite occupants—take a more active role in the identification and recruitment of diverse candidates.

Most executives have a long way to go to make this a reality in their organizations. While the Deloitte study discussed earlier revealed that employees today value diversity and inclusion—so much so that they would be willing to leave their current organiza-

---

49   Jeanne Meister, "The Future of Work: Three New HR Roles in the Age of Artificial Intelligence," *Forbes*, September 24, 2018, https://www.forbes.com/sites/jeannemeister/2018/09/24/the-future-of-work-three-new-hr-roles-in-the-age-of-artificial-intelligence/#7c9e0e2d4cd9.

tion for one with a more inclusive culture—they do not believe that their organizations' leaders hold these ideals in the same esteem. Most workers believe that while inclusion is touted as a company value, it is not considered to be a business imperative.[50]

Since we know diversity is essential to success—and that employees want to see their leaders actively embrace inclusion—it is time for senior executives to get on board and demonstrate their dedication to this vital cause throughout their organizations, rather than siloing various diversity concerns under departments such as HR or legal. That crucial involvement begins with hiring and continues throughout every aspect of a company—from technology infrastructure to available accommodations and company culture. With that in mind, let's discuss how to create an environment that supports diverse employees and encourages individual success for the benefit of the organization at large.

---

50   Deloitte, "The Inclusion Imperative: Redefining Leadership," *Wall Street Journal*, September 4, 2018, https://deloitte.wsj.com/cio/2018/09/04/the-inclusion-imperative-redefining-leadership/https://deloitte.wsj.com/cio/2018/09/04/the-inclusion-imperative-redefining-leadership/.

CHAPTER 6
Respecting Every Human's Ability to Make a Difference: Don't Let Discomfort Hold You Back

W hen I began working in IBM's Human Ability and Accessibility Center, I quickly realized that IBM's approach to accessibility aligned with its insights on diversity at large. Rather than being housed under HR—as accessibility-related initiatives are in many organizations—the Accessibility Center falls under the auspices of IBM Research.

This organizational structure leads to a distinctly different perspective. It means that the progress and decisions IBM makes regarding access have less in common with typical HR considerations like compliance. Rather, they are akin to those accompanying research. Research is about innovation. It's about building the future, and that in and of itself sets the expectation that when IBM brings people into its Accessibility Center, the company respects their ability to contribute to its research goals. In turn, employees know they are not there to fill a quota but to change the way the world works today and tomorrow.

Prior to joining the Accessibility Center, I hadn't had any experience with accessibility, and by the same token, I didn't have any preconceived notions about it. Rather than approach my work with thoughts of compliance or concerns about my team's capabilities or limitations, I walked in with a research mindset: curiosity and a willingness to learn.

I remember attending my first conference on disability, the annual California State University at Northridge (CSUN) Assistive Technology Conference. The biggest conference on assistive technology in the world, the CSUN Assistive Technology conference brings together researchers, practitioners, users, and other stakeholders to explore technological and practical solutions to accessibility-related issues those with disabilities face academically, professionally, and socially.[51]

On the other side of those conference doors was a world that I had never before experienced. I was blown away by the wealth of assistive technology out there, as well as the ways attendees were using it to process information. Some people sat with guide dogs by their sides, typing away on a Braille display. Others were listening to the web through their screen readers at extremely high speeds. The words were coming so fast that I couldn't make them out, because—as I later discovered—many people with limited or no vision learn to compensate with much faster sound processing. And among the conference-goers was Stevie Wonder, checking out the latest developments in accessible technology. A frequent CSUN conference attendee, he is deeply committed to incorporating these advances into his music-making process and helping others enjoy music and other art forms through accessible tools.

---

51 CSUN Division of Student Affairs and Center on Disabilities, "Conference," accessed October 11, 2018, https://www.csun.edu/cod/conference.

NECESSARY ADAPTABILITY FOSTERS EXCEPTIONAL CAPABILITY

I was also amazed by the creativity, talent, and ingenuity of my colleagues. Dr. Dimitri Kanevsky, for example, was one of the research scientists on my team. An extraordinary inventor, he holds more than 150 patents and was named a Master Inventor—an IBM designation given to those who have made an exceptional impact on the world through their patents—in 2002, 2005, and 2010.[52]

As a deaf person, much of Kanevsky's work seeks to improve access for those facing similar obstacles. Among his many groundbreaking inventions are the first Russian automatic speech-recognition system; a vibration-based hearing aid; speech-recognition communication aids that function over the phone; the first internet-based stenographic services; the ViaScribe system, which creates real-time transcriptions and notes from lectures; and technology to incorporate speech recognition into cars, to name just a handful.[53] I am grateful to have had the opportunity to work on a few patents with him, including our most recent project, an automated educational system that can identify any difficulties a user may have with the material, convey those challenges to the user and/or another party, and offer new or modified lessons based on the issues the user is having.[54] In 2012, President Obama named Kanevsky a Champion of Change for his remarkable efforts to improve education and employment opportunities in STEM for Americans with disabilities.[55] Today, he is sharing his talents as a research scientist at Google.

---

52   "Champions of Change: Winning the Future Across America," The White House, accessed October 11, 2018, https://obamawhitehouse.archives.gov/champions/ stem-equality-for-americans-with-disabilities/dimitri-kanevsky.

53   "Champions of Change."

54   Sara Basson, Robert Farrell, Dimitri Kanevsky, and Frances West, "Automated Educational System," US Patent 10049593, filed July 15, 2013, and issued August 14, 2018.

55   "Champions of Change."

Kanevsky's personal need to adapt to the world around him led to his focus on understanding and advancing speech technology and drives his capacity to innovate. As a result, he has made tremendous contributions not only to IBM but also to the world at large.

Another team member, Matt King, provided invaluable insight to help IBM identify issues and come up with solutions to make mobile content, the web, and the workplace more accessible globally. As a blind software engineer, he was able to share his perspective on both the creation and use of accessible technology. He is currently at Facebook, working to provide a more complete experience for blind users and all those who access the platform.

His latest project at Facebook tackles a new issue that has developed alongside the explosion of social media: making the overwhelming abundance of user-generated content more accessible. In the past, when companies controlled the vast majority of content on the Internet, a communications department might have tagged a company's images, clicking through and labeling people, cats, mountains—anything an image might contain for detection by screen readers. Now, anyone can self-publish, and labeling the massive amounts of images out there by hand would be impossible.

But machine learning has the capacity to tag those objects, and Matt is leading the charge to do this at Facebook. After being fed millions of images, AI can discern the contents of an image—labeling dogs, people, even the sunglasses on their faces. Now, technology can do even more, determining not only that an image contains a dog but also that the dog is happy. On a ubiquitous platform where the majority of content is user-generated, Matt's work enables so many more people to participate in meaningful ways.[56]

56   Seth Fiegerman, "Facebook's First Blind Engineer Is Revolutionizing Social Media As We Know It," Mashable, April 5, 2016. https://mashable.com/2016/04/05/matt-king-facebook/#Lk5Ao7WDfOqZ.

Another brilliant scientist I had the privilege of working with at IBM is Chieko Asakawa. Her technical inventions span decades. From her work in the 1980s developing digital Braille systems that are still in use today, to the IBM Home Page Reader—a transformative voice browser that helped make the internet accessible for the blind—and innovations that are helping blind users experience the growing presence of multimedia content on the web, she has been instrumental in improving the digital tools available to people with low or no vision.[57]

Her inventions also help programmers and designers to build more accessible products. One tool that she and her team created, the aDesigner, simulates disabilities to help developers spot potential issues with a product or program's usability during the design process.[58] Asakawa has garnered recognition around the world for her work. Her latest Ted Talk, "How New Technology Helps Blind People," has nearly 1.3 million views. She has also been named an IBM Fellow, the company's highest award for technical accomplishment. Among those who have received this distinction are five Nobel Laureates, five Turing Award winners, a Kyoto Prize winner, and a US Presidential Medal of Freedom winner.[59] To date, she is the only blind technologist to achieve this recognition.

INVESTING IN EVERYONE'S ABILITY TO INVENT THE FUTURE

Working with such brilliant practitioners was tremendously inspiring. It also instilled in me the desire to help the business world understand

---

57 "Chieko Asakawa," IBM, accessed November 1, 2018, https://researcher.watson.ibm.com/researcher/view.php?person=us-chiekoa.

58 "Chieko Asakawa."

59 "IBM Fellows: Extraordinary Achievements by Exceptional Individuals," IBM, accessed November 1, 2018, https://www.ibm.com/ibm/ideasfromibm/us/ibm_fellows/.

that we are not talking about compliance or charity here. People with disabilities are not only capable of succeeding but also far exceeding expectations and performing at the highest levels to help companies invent the future. This ability comes from a need to problem-solve for themselves—creating their own adaptive behaviors and accommodations—and leads to disruptive ideas that serve us all.

Enabling all talented employees to realize the fullest extent of their potential requires a workplace that is inclusive and accessible in every sense of the word, from the foundational physical structures necessary to reach the front door to the online infrastructure that allows our employees to change the world.

INNOVATION FOR PARITY AND PRODUCTIVITY

While investing in every aspect of organizational infrastructure—physical, digital, and cultural—is key to creating equal access and opportunity, much of what we are seeing in today's business world is companies working to identify diverse talent more efficiently through technology. To do this, some businesses are expanding the role of HR. They are embedding technology into their departments to make this traditionally human-focused sector more analytical. For example, Kraft Heinz is adding HR positions that focus on people and data analytics to its slate of traditional positions. The company's senior vice president of global HR, Melissa Werneck, explained that "having a combined responsibility for people and IT functions allows us to complement the people function with activities that are traditionally exclusive to IT, like leveraging machine-learning techniques and using sophisticated algorithms to automate work."[60] However, with more

---

60   Jeanne Meister, "The Future of Work: Three New HR Roles in
       the Age of Artificial Intelligence," *Forbes*, September 24, 2018,
       https://www.forbes.com/sites/jeannemeister/2018/09/24/
       the-future-of-work-three-new-hr-roles-in-the-age-of-artificial-intelligence/#1f14ea5f4cd9.

technology tools in play, HR risks becoming less human—making it harder for companies to find people with unique talents who can make the kinds of changes that will support disruptive innovation.

To fully operationalize this reality, individuals at every level and in every department of a company must get involved. Everyone is looking for the next greenfield opportunity, and the population of people with disabilities—1.3 billion individuals around the world—is just that. People with disabilities go to the bank, shop for groceries, and seek out entertainment just like everyone else. That makes accessibility a vital issue for any CMO. It's an issue for the CIO too since accessible technology in the workplace is necessary to help people with disabilities do their jobs—and provide the kind of insight that can help the business create or to compete in the market we just discussed.

When I first began working in accessibility at IBM, collaborating with HR was not my first priority. Most of my time was spent with the product teams to make sure everything coming out of IBM would serve all of our customers as best and as accessibly as possible. That kind of focus is a differentiator, leading to revenue generation and protecting the company from risk factors like lawsuits. I also spent much of my time collaborating with the CIO's office, working to make every employee's internal IT experience accessible and supportive.

As organizations begin to think about broadening their approach to accessibility and inclusion, they should be strategic. Since no company has unlimited resources, it's crucial to prioritize the initiatives that make the most impact. One of the first things we did when I became director of the Accessibility Center was hold a global summit at IBM, bringing together employees from different disability constituencies to determine our most pressing issues. Blind employees, deaf employees, those with cognitive differences, and those facing mobility challenges gathered with company leaders for a multiple-day meeting to discuss the impact of technology on various disabilities. From there, we determined our priorities.

Of course, we couldn't enact every idea we generated. But together, we were able to prioritize and choose the initiatives that would add the most value. We all agreed that a common accommodation process would offer significant benefits. What does that mean?

Well, previously, if a first-line manager wanted to hire a candidate who was blind, the manager would have to start from scratch: identifying, learning, and purchasing the technology necessary to help that individual do his or her job, piece by piece. We realized that if there were an online system in play to help managers identify and implement necessary accommodations with just a few clicks, it would streamline the process.

So, we developed the Workplace Accommodation Connection system. Now, when a manager is bringing on board someone with a disability, they can simply head to the accommodation website and enter information about employee needs. Because of IBM's experience working with people with disabilities, the system knows that a blind employee will need a screen reader, specialized software that turns text into speech. It knows that those who are deaf may benefit from American Sign Language services. The system can then order any product or service necessary so that when the employee arrives at the office for his or her first day, the technology they need to thrive is already in place. And most important, the system is also designed to be self-serve: an employee can procure the necessary product or services online, without the involvement or approval of a manager or anybody else. By the way, a central budget covers the cost of this system, so no individual department has to worry about the financial impact of procuring accommodation.

It was a multiyear, multimillion-dollar project, but it was worth it. We put in the money, the resources, and the skills, and as a result, IBM can hire a person anywhere throughout the world and ensure they have the tools they need to operate successfully from day one.

In addition to implementing the required accommodations, with the Workplace Accommodation Connection system, IBM has built an environment that makes doing so easy and intuitive, incorporating parity and productivity into every employee's experience. This is the epitome of a systematic approach, and it makes scaling and sustaining the company's values possible because they are actually built into the company infrastructure. It's not about creating a separate but equal path; it's about ensuring the same road can carry us all toward success—and technology like the Workplace Accommodation Connection system allows us to do just that.

Since the system was developed, IBM has open-sourced the program to make it available to other organizations. And now, there's an app for that. In 2016, IBM partnered with the Center for Disability Inclusion at West Virginia University and the Job Accommodation Network (JAN)—a nonprofit funded by the US Department of Labor that provides comprehensive information and support on workplace accessibility and accommodations—to further develop this technology for a broader reach.[61]

With a federal research grant from the National Institute on Disability, Independent Living, and Rehabilitation Research, they developed the Mobile Accommodation Solution (MAS). Based on IBM's own internal system, MAS is a mobile app that manages organizations' accommodation requests from applicants, candidates, and

---

61   Job Accommodation Network, "About JAN," accessed October 11, 2018, https://askjan. org/about-us/index.cfm.

employees.[62] MAS is now a free app available for iOS devices.

With tools like these readily available, the average cost of implementing individual accommodations in your own workplace is actually quite low, if anything at all, and has major benefits. A study by JAN and the University of Iowa's Law, Health Policy, and Disability Center found that most workplace accommodations cost less than $500. In addition, "employers reported that providing accommodations resulted in such benefits as retaining valuable employees, improving productivity and morale, reducing workers' compensation and training costs, and improving company diversity."[63]

BUILDING A CULTURE OF ACCOMMODATION TO BENEFIT ALL

Systems like this one also come with derivative benefits that go beyond the original purpose of the design. For example, after setting up IBM's accommodation system, we started getting calls from our ergonomics department, asking whether we could incorporate accommodations for those with work-related injuries, such as back pain or carpal tunnel syndrome, into the system. Now, multiple departments can use this common infrastructure to accomplish their goal of helping employees more efficiently.

Sometimes I see companies engage people with disabilities with great intentions. But because their orientation is usually from a social responsibility or philanthropic angle, they can miss the key point that creating an infrastructure for sustainable operations is essential. Bringing on one or two people with disabilities at a time will not

---

62   Peter Fay, "Enhancing the Reasonable Accommodation Process in the Workplace," IBM, September 8, 2017, https://www.ibm.com/blogs/age-and-ability/2017/09/08/enhancing-reasonable-accommodation-process-workplace/.
63   Benefits and Costs of Accommodation," Job Accommodation Network, accessed November 1, 2018, https://askjan.org/topics/costs.cfm.

sustain or scale, as it is a one-off effort. Such an approach may even create the unintentional negative outcome of putting people with disabilities on a pedestal and treating them like superheroes—a potentially isolating and uncomfortable position to be in.

The more I work in the accessibility field, the more I have come to believe there is a tremendous upside to having many people with different abilities in the workplace. Picture a bell curve. Most people fall somewhere in the middle—they're of "normal" intelligence or ability, and the vast majority of the world is designed with them in mind. But when you design for the extremes—the thinkers, workers, and players at the edges of the curve—you spur inventions that work better for all of us. This is the vast potential of universal, or extreme-case, design. It will help us account for the issues we'll face tomorrow and create technology that can adapt to the needs of every user.

We encounter examples of universal design and its widespread benefits every day. Consider the curb cut on almost every street corner, a design function originally implemented to accommodate wheelchairs. Once in place, it became obvious that the curb cut helped us all get across the street more smoothly and safely in one situation or another—whether pushing a baby stroller, pulling heavy luggage, or using crutches or a cane for an injury. The accessible technology of today will be the universal standard of tomorrow, and getting on board now means leading the future, rather than struggling to keep up.

IT'S NOT ABOUT "THEM," IT'S ABOUT ALL OF US

There is another aspect of accessibility that makes it both universally important and an often-uncomfortable topic. Unlike the specific traits that mark other diversity groups—which those in the majority are often able to distance themselves from—disability could happen to any of us, at any point.

And as we age, a certain level of deterioration becomes par for the course. For instance, while about 15 percent of the general population has a disability, for those over fifty, the rate is 25 percent. By the time we reach sixty-five, more than half of us will have a disability. Whether or not you have a disability right now, it is likely that you will face some kind of mental or physical challenge as you age—meaning the accessibility protocols we develop today are not just for "them," they're for all of us.[64]

This issue is gaining in importance as the world's population is aging more quickly than ever. It is estimated that by 2050, for the first time in human history, there will be more older people on the planet than younger ones—a demographic shift that has already occurred in a number of countries, including Japan, Italy, and Germany.[65] With age comes a shift in our needs and in the accommodations all of us will need to work and live. When we recognize this trend, the need to invest in technology that enables everyone's participation becomes even clearer. But we must also understand that this is a long-term investment.

TRUE INCLUSION TAKES PATIENCE

All those years ago, when Frank Friedersdorf gave me a job, he didn't just see what I could do in that moment; he saw what I could accomplish in the future. Creating a culture of Authentic Inclusion doesn't happen overnight. Shifting our thinking, and changing the culture of a company at large, requires patience.

In the early part of the twentieth century, very few buildings had an elevator for use by the public—companies just had stairs. If you

---

64   Laura Langendorf, "#AccessibleOlli Drives Us Forward at CES," IBM Internet of Things Blog, January 12, 2018, https://www.ibm.com/blogs/internet-of-things/iot-accessibleolli-drives-us-forward-at-ces/.

65   "Outthink Aging: Explore the Challenges and Opportunities Created by an Aging Society," IBM Corporation, 2016, https://www.giaging.org/documents/IBM_16_09.PDF.

did need to use one, you might find an elevator designed to transport freight, traveling through garages, back alleys, and other nonpublic spaces to arrive at your destination. Since then, the elevator has been designed primarily to transport people rather than heavy objects, and it serves everyone, whether they use it out of necessity or convenience. More important, and as the Americans with Disabilities Act of 1990 ensures, those who have disabilities don't have to take a separate route just to get to the same place.

Today, the answers to access limitations and opportunities often lie in technology. To address them, the Partnership on Employment and Accessible Technology (PEAT), an organization funded by the US Department of Labor's Office of Disability Employment Policy, is working to help companies understand the value of investing in accessible tech in addition to talented and diverse employees.

In 2018, PEAT partnered with Teach Access—an organization that encourages academic institutions to incorporate the concept of universal design into curricula for researchers, computer scientists, and designers—to conduct a survey on the current state of accessibility in the workplace. Results revealed that while 93 percent of respondents shared that the demand for accessibility-related skills is growing, 63 percent reported that their staff doesn't have the skills necessary to achieve their goals, and 60 percent said they found it "difficult" or "very difficult" to identify and hire new talent who could bridge the gap.[66] It will take time to remedy this deficiency— and a commitment to starting with the education students receive and to hiring inclusively from the beginning. In the meantime, we can ensure that we are putting systems in place to attract highly

---

66   Lisa Morgan, "Good Tech Design Is Accessible, But There's a
      Skills Gap," *InformationWeek*, October 10, 2018, https://www.
      informationweek.com/strategic-cio/team-building-and-staffing/
      good-tech-design-is-accessible-but-theres-a-skills-gap/a/d-id/1332994.

qualified candidates with disabilities, support employees who need accommodations, and create accessibility training for those tasked with enhancing the workplace environment and its resources. Much of that can be accomplished through technology.

ACCESSIBLE INFRASTRUCTURE IS ESSENTIAL

The Kessler Foundation's 2017 National Employment and Disability Survey confirms the essential nature of this priority with input from more than 3,000 supervisors around the country. Responses indicated that there are numerous opportunities to improve the workplace environment for all employees through technology, though few organizations are harnessing them. For example, a centralized accommodation fund, like the one we discussed earlier in this chapter, was shown to be 97 percent effective in expanding opportunities for those with disabilities, but only 16 percent of employers have them.[67]

Just as with hiring, to turn this tide and make sure all employees have the infrastructure necessary to contribute, members of the executive suite need to weigh in. As Kessler Foundation president and CEO Rodger DeRose said, "When there is commitment from upper management, and effective practices are in place, all employees and their supervisors achieve success, and businesses reap the benefits of their diverse and productive workforce."[68]

---

67 "National Survey Provides New Directions for Expanding Inclusion of People with Disabilities in the Workplace: Kessler Foundation Releases Results of First-of-its-Kind Survey," Kessler Foundation press release, October 10, 2017, https://kesslerfoundation.org/kfsurvey17/pressrelease.
68 "National Survey Provides New Directions."

YOU CAN'T GET COMFORTABLE IF YOU CAN'T GET PHYSICAL

The key to creating an accessible workplace environment is understanding the needs, interests, and goals of people with disabilities. In his book *Hit Refresh: The Quest to Rediscover Microsoft's Soul and Imagine a Better Future for Everyone*, Microsoft CEO Satya Nadella writes about how having a son with special needs informs his work at Microsoft. He writes, "Becoming a father of a son with special needs was the turning point in my life that has shaped who I am today. It has helped me better understand the journey of people with disabilities. It has shaped my personal passion for and philosophy of connecting new ideas to empathy for others. And it is why I am deeply committed to pushing the bounds on what love and compassion combined with human ingenuity and passion to have impact can accomplish with my colleagues at Microsoft."[69] While many of us don't have the same firsthand experience with disability that Nadella does, we can all work to connect with those different from us and thus better understand how to best support them.

Engaging with constituents often raises the same issue many leaders face when discussing disability in general: discomfort. Many of us find ourselves failing to make our organizations more accessible because we are uncomfortable with the subject of disability—and, perhaps, even more uneasy about interacting with those who have one. We don't know how to talk about it, so we don't. But talking about it and taking action are necessary for the welfare of ourselves, our organizations, and our society at large. And if we don't choose to engage with it directly, we'll never achieve the kind of progress we

---

69   Satya Nadella, "The Moment That Forever Changed Our Lives," LinkedIn, October 21, 2017, https://www.linkedin.com/pulse/moment-forever-changed-our-lives-satya-nadella/.

want, financially or otherwise. There's a Chinese saying that goes, "It's like trying to scratch your itchy points through your boots." In other words, without true engagement, you can't hit the right spot. You just keep circling, circling, and circling around again, but you never get to the heart of the matter. It's time to take off our boots.

Bringing Authentic Inclusion to fruition requires getting comfortable, and that means you must interact with and get to know those you hope to serve. You cannot get comfortable if you cannot get physical—meaning face-to-face meetings with the various constituencies in your workplace are a necessity.

That first CSUN Assistive Technology Conference helped open my eyes to the world around me because I was able to better understand the experience of some of the people I would be working with. It enabled me to interact with others on a human level and understand how we could work together to meet our goals. Similarly, I recently spoke at an Amazing Community event for women over fifty called Inclusion by Design (https://www.inclusionbydesign.org/). The event would serve as an eye-opener to anyone who might imagine that women over fifty are sitting at home, getting ready to become grandmothers. Instead, the room was filled with highly skilled and professionally accomplished women who are keen on continuing to learn and grow their understanding of new concepts.

Inclusion is such a big topic now that you could attend large-scale conferences like these once a week, encountering diverse attendees and potentially learning from their presentations. But perhaps more effective than sitting in a huge audience, hearing about the benefits of inclusion—many of which you likely know—is to participate in a smaller, more engaged environment and actually sit down with someone with a different set of experiences and abilities than your own.

This kind of setting often brings admiration for others' capabilities and a deeper understanding of their experiences and what they can bring to the table.

One innovative practice that has had a profound effect on some of the most progressive companies, including IBM, is called "reverse mentoring." In this practice, executives were paired with employees with disabilities so that members of the senior leadership team could see how members of their teams worked on a daily basis, using the numerous technology tools that allowed them to be productive and successful. Reverse mentoring and the relationships it generated allowed both parties to better understand each other's perspective and deepened executives' understanding of, and belief in, the value of different abilities and accessibility at large.

This approach can be extended to anyone at your company whose experience differs from the majority. For instance, if your organization is primarily composed of men, you may want to hold a roundtable with women. Further, bringing in women of different levels and backgrounds—not just those who are considered to be the company's rising stars—will add to the depth of your understanding, and potentially lead to new policies and accommodations that will help them contribute to your organization.

The more technologically driven our society becomes, the more human engagement matters. So many tech companies and their leaders are only comfortable talking about tech, big data analytics, and the like; they're not comfortable talking about humans. But when it comes to Artificial Intelligence—programming computers to think like humans—it's imperative that we remember that the true purpose of our work is to improve the lives of *people*. With that in mind, we can create stronger connections, and better products, services, and experiences for all.

CHAPTER 7
Aligning Principle, Purpose, and Profit: The Great Way

In 2016, I retired from IBM after thirty-plus years with the company. I spent the last third of my time working in accessibility, and those years were some of the most fulfilling of my career. But it was only after turning in my badge and IBM computer that I realized exactly why I was so passionate about my time with the Human Ability and Accessibility Center and my subsequent role as Chief Accessibility Officer.

During my tenure, people would ask me about why I was so dedicated to my work, and I had a bevy of answers. Sometimes, I told them it was because accessibility is at the crux of technology's increasing role in all of our lives—serving more human purposes and simultaneously taking on more human traits than ever before—and thus it was up to me to help make sure our people and products reflected that shift. Other times, I told them that as a first-generation female minority, I understood accessibility as a human rights issue and could empathize with the need to be included. While they were certainly true, these answers lacked something I couldn't put my finger on.

They didn't quite get to the heart of the matter for me.

One day, shortly after I retired, I was going through some old books that I had read over the years. I came across an old essay by Confucius. The title translates to "The Great Way" or "The Great Together."[70] In this essay, Confucius explains that the ultimate society is one that belongs to the public. It's a place where each person has a place and where everyone is cared for—regardless of his or her abilities. As a result, everyone has what he or she needs. The concept was very organic to me, as it is imparted upon all children growing up in Taiwan. I quickly realized that this childhood lesson had been fueling my purpose at work and beyond. The Great Way had lived in my unconscious all these years, and I had been doing my part to try to fulfill it.

In a true democratic society, everyone is created equal. As a result, all of the people in it have the right to dream of a better future. They have equal access to opportunity. They have the tools to work toward a better quality of life and to find happiness. Practicing The Great Way helps all of us succeed—not just some of us. And we can all do our part to bring ourselves, and our world, closer to greatness. When we operate with a real sense of purpose—one that is driven by a human-first sensibility—and create processes, policies, and products that reflect that, everybody wins.

A SENSE OF PURPOSE DRIVES SUCCESS

In his 2017 commencement speech at MIT Sloan School of Management, Apple CEO Tim Cook discussed the challenge and power of purpose. He shared that he had had a lifetime of difficulty finding his purpose; he had failed to uncover it as a child, in college and

---

70   Confucius, "'The Great Together (Li Yun Da Tong)' from the Chapter 'The Operation of Etiquette' in Li Ji," trans. Feng Xin-ming, April 2008, http://tsoidug.org/Literary/Etiquette_Great_Together_Simp.pdf.

graduate school, and through meditation and religion. It was only after joining Apple, a company with a strong sense of purpose, that "it finally clicked."[71]

Apple's purpose, to serve humanity, was integral to Cook's ability to discover his own. And it was this sense of alignment that helped him realize a core truth: "If you choose to live your lives at that intersection between technology and the people it serves, if you strive to create the best, give the best, do the best for everyone, not just for some, then today all of humanity has good cause for hope."[72] As our culture and our connections to technology and each other grow more complex, our purpose must become simpler and more prominent: to serve everyone.

Among the many shifting aspects of our society is the answer to an important question: *Who is responsible for the welfare of humanity?* The government no longer provides the same level of support for marginalized members of society, and nonprofits don't have the capacity to pick up all of the slack. As such, society is increasingly turning to the private sector and asking companies to respond to the broader challenges we face today. To address them, we have to institutionalize practices that meet the needs of all people, investing in infrastructure and developing new technologies that put all humans first. This commitment is part and parcel of success.

Larry Fink, chairman and CEO of BlackRock, elaborated on this powerful point in his annual letter to CEOs, laying out some of society's most pressing issues, and with them the increasing "[demand] that companies, both public and private, serve a social

---

71   Molly Rubin, "Full Transcript: Tim Cook Delivers MIT's 2017 Commencement Speech," Quartz, June 9, 2017, https://qz.com/1002570/watch-live-apple-ceo-tim-cook-delivers-mits-2017-commencement-speech/.
72   Rubin, "Full Transcript."

purpose."[73] Fink wrote, "Companies must ask themselves: What role do we play in the community? How are we managing our impact on the environment? Are we working to create a diverse workforce? Are we adapting to technological change? Are we providing the retraining and opportunities that our employees and our business will need to adjust to an increasingly automated world?"

AN ACT OF KINDNESS CAN DIFFERENTIATE: TJ MAXX'S STORY

Part of this work involves embodying a characteristic that's not quite quantifiable: authenticity. While authenticity is hard to measure in terms of metrics, the benefits are concrete. Consider the case of off-price store TJ Maxx. You may know it for its impressive selection, low prices, great return policy, and excellent customer service, but it's the company's holistically human-centric approach that makes it particularly successful. Retail business margins are very slim, so it's crucial that the company's buyers are able to negotiate and get the best bargains.

But rather than hiring the shrewdest negotiators, TJ Maxx hires the nicest, most authentic people to be its buyers, and unlike many other retail companies, it trains them. In addition to an education in consumer and fashion trends and pricing at TJX University—the company's training program—buyers are taught about the value of relationships. "We want the way we do business—with integrity, honesty, and caring about one another—to continue to permeate our culture, and we speak to this within our program," said Carol

73   Larry Fink, "Larry Fink's Annual Letter to CEOs: A Sense of Purpose,"
      BlackRock, accessed October 11, 2018, https://www.blackrock.com/
      corporate/investor-relations/larry-fink-ceo-letter?cid=twitter%3Alarryslettertoc
      eos%3A%3Ablackrock.

Meyrowitz, the company's executive chairman of the board and chairman of the executive committee of TJX Companies, which includes Marshalls, HomeGoods, and Sierra Trading Post.

When buyers go overseas to source goods from the company's sixteen thousand vendors, they take this human-first approach, forming connections with manufacturers and vendors on a person-to-person level.[74] Because they simply like the buyers as people, the vendors save the best merchandise and prices for them. TJ Maxx is committed to maintaining a human touch throughout the supply chain, and those humans are actually making the difference in terms of profit.

A NEW WAY OF THINKING: PRIORITIZING A RETURN ON INNOVATION

In Chapter 4, we discussed the psychological shifts necessary to embody a human-first mindset. As we begin to ask the questions that bring us closer to our purpose—serving all humans better—we should make yet another shift: valuing return on innovation alongside a return on investment. Prioritizing return on investment alone is a very operational view of business potential: *What can I spend and what can I bring back?* But focusing on return on innovation holds that, because we are looking at areas or populations that have historically been underserved, we need a different kind of metric.

The whole idea behind return on innovation is that you have to invest in the future. Since that proposition inevitably involves humans, and thus more unknowns, the return might take longer at first, or even be less tangible. However, though the payoff may be harder to quantify, it will be significant and ultimately essential to

---

74   Carol Meyrowitz, "The CEO of TJX on How to Train First-Class Buyers," *Harvard Business Review*, May 2014, https://hbr.org/2014/05/the-ceo-of-tjx-on-how-to-train-first-class-buyers.

future success. Perhaps, for instance, if you embrace an authentic set of values as a leader, you'll end up being revered by younger generations, and that level of respect and admiration will help you attract and retain the top talent who will conceive of and launch your next big idea.

IBM Brazil experienced a similar boon when I was working with it to set up an accessibility center there. Because of IBM's dedication to diversity and accessibility, the company was able to secure a substantial research grant to support the project. With the backing to roll out a corresponding study on educating and training people with disabilities for employment, we attracted the very best research talent to carry out the study.

Everything we've discussed about legislation, societal interests, changing demographics, and the current and future frontiers of technology highlights the human-centric nature of our world. People can't only be considered; they must be at the center of everything we do. While the ROI might not be obvious at first, have the foresight to trust that investing in humanity is worth the expense.

UNIVERSAL DESIGN BETTERS EXPERIENCE FOR ALL

From electronic home devices like Alexa to the voice navigation in cars and the controls on our everyday appliances, designers have to consider every human who might be using them. The iPhone offers a great example of combining design thinking with accessibility. Rather than being an afterthought, accessibility is a core part of the process. As head of Apple's accessibility programs, Sarah Herrlinger explains, "We've built accessibility into the guts of our products. . . They're deeply embedded in the OS. It's built in, not bolted on."[75]

---

75   Rachel Kraus, "8 Useful iPhone Accessibility Features You Might Not Know About," Mashable, May 17, 2018, https://mashable.com/2018/05/17/iphone-accessibility-features-for-everyone/#.ui6eMIVAaqX.

As a result, iPhone continues to set the standard for accessibility. For instance, the phone has multiple features that support individuals with color blindness and low vision, including the option to increase contrast, alter brightness, augment the size of text, and even magnify print. One can also turn on captioning so that whenever captions are available in an app, they will appear—a benefit for those who are deaf or hard of hearing. In addition, Siri, Apple's digital assistant, allows people with mobility challenges and other disabilities to complete tasks with just the sound of their voices.[76]

These features can help all of us in different scenarios where our functioning is limited due to the environment, such as attempting to read the small print of a restaurant menu, absorbing video content in a loud place, or using voice commands when hands are otherwise occupied. Instances like these are sometimes referred to as "situational disabilities," and we've all experienced them at one time or another, further driving home the universal benefits that occur when accessibility is at the heart of design.

In addition to bettering individuals' everyday functional experiences, organizations are also capitalizing on technology to improve recreational experiences for all. The United Kingdom's National Theatre has invested in the experience of its deaf and hard-of-hearing theatergoers with smart glasses. The technology, which augments the viewers' surroundings with images and information based on their environment, never really caught on with the general public in the way its creators anticipated. But it is improving the theater experience for those with hearing loss.

National Theatre ticketholders can call ahead and request a pair of Epson Moverio BT-350s, which the theater refers to as "Smart Caption Glasses." The glasses provide a text description of dialogue

---

76   Kraus, "8 Useful iPhone Accessibility Features."

and sound effects in real time, as the user tracks the action on stage. The glasses also have the option for extreme personalization, with a menu to select the size, color, and placement of text for optimal enjoyment.[77] And, as with most instances of extreme-case design, the smart glasses also have the potential to benefit other groups, such as non-English-speaking attendees, who could use these valuable tools to better understand the on-stage dialog and have a more enriching theater-going experience.

A startup called Aira—to which I am an advisor—is also capitalizing on smart glasses and smartphone technology to serve people with disabilities. Through the service, blind and low-vision individuals can share their surroundings with sighted agents, who can help them navigate their environment and complete tasks like reading their mail, using otherwise inaccessible technology, and finding their way through a store or an airport.[78]

Aira also provides a massive opportunity to address the extremely high unemployment rate for blind and low-vision individuals—which is around 70 percent—and support visually impaired entrepreneurs.[79] Recently, Intuit, a financial software company, offered the service to all entrepreneurs and small-business owners, with the goal of decreasing the unemployment rate and improving lives.[80] Like the smart glasses used by the National Theatre, this technology also offers benefits to the general population in a variety of situations, such as trying to navigate airports and locations in other countries, where they do not speak the language.

---

77   Henry St. Leger, "AR Meets Accessibility: How Epson's Smart Glasses Found a Home in the Theater," Techradar, October 11, 2018, https://www.techradar.com/news/ar-meets-accessibility-how-epsons-smart-glasses-found-a-home-in-the-theater.

78   Leigh Buchanan, "This Company's Technology 'Sees' for Blind Entrepreneurs," *Inc.*, October 19, 2018, https://www.inc.com/leigh-buchanan/aira-blind-entrepreneurs-tool.html.

79   Buchanan, "This Company's Technology."

80   Buchanan, "This Company's Technology."

This kind of thinking can extend beyond individual businesses. For instance, the cities of Chicago and New York are working to cultivate a culture of accessibility as part of the Inclusive Innovation for Smarter Cities project. Led by G3ict and World Enabled, a consulting group focused on building "inclusive societies where people with disabilities can fully develop their talents and reach their full potential," the project aims to increase cities' accessibility for people with disabilities and the aging by decreasing the digital divide.[81], [82] Through this effort, Chicago and New York are working to differentiate themselves by providing all city dwellers—including older people and those with disabilities—with better tools while grooming the next generation of startups to be more accessibility aware.[83] These cities are not only investing in the infrastructure that allows people with disabilities to get on a train or bus but also in a slate of ventures that have all citizens' needs and wants in mind. By embracing accessibility as a business imperative, the cities, and all those served by the project, set themselves apart.

In October 2018, I had the privilege of participating as a subject matter expert in Chicago's first Inclusive Innovation Roundtable, a gathering of government officials, industry leaders, and disability advocates. Our group discussed how the city could help startups incorporate accessibility from the start, pairing entrepreneurs with experts who can explain the benefits of designing their web applications, marketing websites, or mobile apps to be more accessible. We also touched on the power of process innovation within the life cycle of a startup, from having a concept to participating in incubators,

---

81   "Leading Organizations," Smart Cities for All, accessed November 8, 2018, http://smartcities4all.org/#leading-organizations.
82   "Smart Cities for All," accessed November 8, 2018, http://smartcities4all.org/.
83   "Innovation Is the Key to Smarter Cities," Smart Cities for All, accessed October 11, 2018, http://smartcities4all.org/innovation-is-the-key-to-smarter-cities/.

embedding accessible concepts and exposure from the very beginning so that founders are constantly thinking about serving all people. The conversation also highlighted the power of user testing, engaging local disability organizations to try out some of the city-based applications to ensure they are actually useful to the populations they are meant to benefit—a vital concept called "designing in."

DESIGNING IN FOR ALL HUMANS

Whether working on behalf of a small startup or a whole city, involving people with different abilities and perspectives is an essential part of the process. This is key to "designing in," a system design process. Designing in is built on three principles: "early and continual focus on users; empirical measurement of usage and iterative design whereby the system . . . is modified, tested, modified again, tested again, and the cycle is repeated again and again."[84]

Many companies are embracing the principles behind designing in, not just for better system efficiency but also for better human experience based on incorporating the latest technology. And they are disrupting their industries in the process. For example, one startup called Navibration is attempting to transform the tourism industry with a product that keeps the needs of blind and visually impaired users in mind with blockchain technology.

Navibration is creating travel guides that can be used on tablets and smartphones. Instead of a visual map, the guides use audio and vibration to direct users. The company also has a series of wearables in the works, including one specifically designed for those with low or no vision: a "Navibration Stick," Navibration technology incorpo-

---

84   John D. Gould and Clayton Lewis, "Designing for Usability: Key Principles and What Designers Think," *Communications of the ACM*, March 1985, https://dl.acm.org/citation.cfm?id=3170.

rated into a walking stick.[85] The guide content is created by users, and by using blockchain, the content creators can also share in the profits generated from sales—a great example of innovative use of design and cutting-edge technology.

Clothing Brand Tommy Hilfiger has launched Tommy Adaptive, a line designed for and with people with disabilities. With elements like magnetic flies, fasteners, and zippers, Tommy Adaptive makes getting dressed easier for those with limited dexterity. The line also includes pants with magnetic leg openings to accommodate leg braces, casts, and orthotics, and clothes designed to be more comfortable for those in wheelchairs.[86]

The company partnered with Runway of Dreams, a nonprofit working to make fashion more accessible to people with disabilities, to create the collection. Runway of Dreams' founder, Mindy Scheier, was inspired to start the organization because of her son Oliver. Oliver has muscular dystrophy, a disease that results in loss of muscle mass and weakness, but he wanted to wear jeans to school, just like his classmates.[87] Since its launch, the foundation has engaged in many activities to improve people with disabilities' access to stylish and functional clothing and the fashion industry at large, including employment, design, and awareness initiatives.

Through Runway of Dreams' partnership with Tommy Hilfiger, the foundation is ensuring that Tommy Hilfiger's clothing line reflects the needs of people with disabilities. In addition, Hilfiger understands the importance of incorporating feedback and iterative design into the products it is developing, with a section on the company's

---

85   Mina Down, "How One Blockchain Startup Is Transforming Travel and Increasing the Accessibility of Cities," Hackernoon, September 30, 2018, https://hackernoon.com/blockchain-social-network-travel-accessibility-660d708dde73.

86   "Tommy Hilfiger Adaptive: Designed with and for People with Disabilities," Tommy Hilfiger, accessed October 11, 2018, https://usa.tommy.com/en/tommy-adaptive.

87   "About," Runway of Dreams Foundation, accessed November 5, 2018, http://runwayof-dreams.org/about/.

website that solicits input from wearers so that people can share what's working, what's not, and what they'd like to see in the future.

Another parent of a child with a disability, Debra Ruh, is also working to get corporations to think about the impact of their messaging and how they can make their branding, products, and services accessible. Debra acknowledges that while few companies are perfect when it comes to accessibility, there is significant value in their willingness to try. Over her social media channels, which have more than 300,000 followers across multiple platforms, she has encouraged people with disabilities and their networks to "reward brands that are doing their best . . . to begin 'voting with our wallets.'"[88] Thanks to efforts like these, and the loyalty of the disability community, Tommy Adaptive has seen success and has expanded from a children's line to one that serves adults as well. This is yet another occasion in which designing for and with one underserved demographic betters the company's bottom line overall.

DESIGN FOR AGING

When we design for and with diverse users, we cannot forget a rapidly growing population that we are all part of: those who are aging. As IBM established in its 2016 "Outthink Aging" report, "The aging population is not a user group. It's a diverse human, global audience with varying needs, habits, technical abilities, and more. Engaging this audience means leveraging technical innovation *and* human empathy to enhance the *human experience.* Technologists must envision and articulate the real advantages of any emerging technology to diverse individuals, communities, and society—as well as to

---

88   Debra Ruh, "Why Corporate Brands Need to Tell Their Inclusion Story and Join the Global B2B Conversations," Talentculture, November 21, 2017, https://talentculture.com/why-corporate-brands-need-to-tell-their-inclusion-story-and-join-the-global-b2b-conversations/.

the marketplace."[89]

When weighing the benefits of incorporating technology into products and services that serve the diverse needs and interests of an aging population, we may find that, in some cases, we need to go retro. For example, many common appliances have gotten pretty high tech, with digital displays that can be very disorienting for older users. I often wonder if my washing machine is getting too smart for me—I want to go back to the old days when I just turned the dial, pushed a button, and knew it was working thanks to the loud clunk of the tub inside. It's easy to fall into the trap of multimodal experiences, building in so many features that simple tasks become confusing. Just because the technology is improving and there are all kinds of interface possibilities doesn't mean the most high-tech one is the best option. Designing in can help avoid some of that.

CAPITALIZING ON TECHNOLOGY'S HUMAN BENEFITS

Other times, we must think about how AI and other complex technologies can serve a human purpose by embodying human traits themselves—especially since our global population is rapidly aging. In the US, ten thousand baby boomers turn sixty-five every day, and approximately 25 percent of China's population will be at least sixty years old by 2030.[90], [91] This reality is making it hard for caregivers to keep up. In 2016, the ratio of available caregivers age forty-five to sixty-four to address the needs of those over age eighty was seven to one; in 2030, the ratio will be just four to one. Technology will have to take over

---

89 "Outthink Aging: Explore the Challenges and Opportunities Created by an Aging Society," IBM Corporation, 2016.
90 Eric Pianin, "10,000 Boomers Turn 65 Every Day. Can Medicare and Social Security Handle It?" *The Fiscal Times*, May 9, 2017.
91 Jing Zhao and Yinan Zhao, "China's Next Debt Bomb Is an Aging Population," Bloomberg, February 5, 2018, https://www.bloomberg.com/news/articles/2018-02-05/china-s-next-debt-bomb-is-an-aging-population.

some of the care responsibilities previously handled by people.[92]

Japan's population is aging rapidly as its workforce is shrinking, meaning that there are fewer workers available to care for its growing elderly population.[93] The country expects a shortage of 380,000 care workers by 2025.[94] One nursing home is addressing this challenge by augmenting its staff with robots, including a seal named Paro. The seal serves as a soft, responsive companion, "[reacting] to touch, speech, and light by moving its head, blinking its eyes, and playing recordings of Canadian harp seal cries."[95] While Paro can't replace workers, it can provide comfort and improve the spirits of nursing home residents. Other robots in use in the nursing home lend a helping hand to employees, including a bed that converts to a wheelchair, a device that helps lift patients, and one that helps patients walk as part of their rehabilitation. The robots' creators believe they will be part of the care solution in many countries that are experiencing a similar demographic shift.

FINDING THE BALANCE BETWEEN MACHINE EFFICIENCY AND HUMAN HAPPINESS

As we implement the many tools at our fingertips to make lives better—whether simple or complex—we have to be sure not to sacrifice human happiness in the process. Today, industry behemoths like Google and Facebook have tremendous data and analytic capabilities, constantly collecting information about users with every click

---

92 "Outthink Aging: Explore the Challenges and Opportunities Created by an Aging Society," IBM Corporation, 2016.

93 Reuters, "Japan's Robot Revolution Helps Care for the Elderly," March 27, 2018, Reuters video, 11:38, https://www.reuters.com/article/us-japan-ageing-robots-widerimage/aging-japan-robots-may-have-role-in-future-of-elder-care-idUSKBN1H33AB.

94 Malcolm Foster, "Aging Japan: Robots May Have Role in Future of Elder Care," March 27, 2018, https://www.reuters.com/article/us-japan-ageing-robots-widerimage/aging-japan-robots-may-have-role-in-future-of-elder-care-idUSKBN1H33AB.

95 Foster, "Aging Japan."

they make, every post they share, and every advertisement they see. The insights platforms like these can offer are incredible. Today's technology enables businesses to reach a "market of one," with analytics so sophisticated that we can predict exactly what a single individual will find most appealing and then encourage them to buy.

There are certainly perks for consumers—I might appreciate it when Instagram offers me a targeted ad with the shoes I've been thinking about at a discounted rate. But while this process may serve customers with hyperpersonalized products and services—and benefit companies' bottom lines—we need to keep an eye on the process itself and the potential of technology to impede its own progress. If I love the shoes an algorithm has selected for me but think my privacy has been compromised in the process, the platform may lose me as a user along with the marketing opportunities that come with me.

According to the Pew Research Center, while 74 percent of people believe it is very important to be in control of their personal data, only 9 percent believe they have "a lot of control" over the information being shared about them through social media.[96] And as people age, they get more nervous about their online safety and security. An AARP survey found that those age fifty and over were more likely to be "very concerned" about the privacy and security of their information than younger adults.[97] With these insights in mind, sites like Facebook should consider what they stand to lose if they don't reconcile the need to collect and monetize data with consumer concerns about privacy.

---

96   Lee Rainie, "American's Complicated Feelings About Social Media in an Era of Privacy Concerns," Pew Research Center, March 27, 2018, http://www.pewresearch.org/fact-tank/2018/03/27/americans-complicated-feelings-about-social-media-in-an-era-of-privacy-concerns/.

97   William Gibson, "Online Privacy a Major Concern, AARP Study Shows," AARP, May 17, 2017, https://www.aarp.org/home-family/personal-technology/info-2017/survey-shows-online-privacy-concerns-fd.html.

I use Facebook because I know enough about it to confidently protect myself. But ten years from now, I may not be as fluent in its privacy settings. If Facebook and similar sites want their companies to have longevity—part of the definition of Authentic Inclusion—then perhaps they should think about the aging population and design a system that can think for me or with me to help protect my privacy at a time when I may not have the capacity or understanding to do it myself. Otherwise, they may risk losing me as a user as soon as my grasp of technology begins to fade.

Meanwhile, companies that choose to take advantage of technology's advances—by, say, changing pricing without anyone realizing—will lose out in the end because those customers won't stick around to be fooled again. For true longevity, purpose and profit have to be aligned. These considerations don't stop with users; they extend to the employees mining the data that powers much of business today. To make for a happier, and more accessible, workplace, we can take lessons from today's "gig economy."

WHAT WE CAN LEARN FROM THE GIG ECONOMY

With around 150 million independent contractors in North America and Western Europe, most everyone agrees that the gig economy is not only here to stay but also here to grow.[98] Historically, it has been underserved populations that have held these so-called "gigs" due to a number of factors conspiring to prevent them from securing full-time jobs. For instance, women and minorities have long staffed door-to-door enterprises like Avon, Tupperware, or Mary Kay. While flexible jobs like these may have been the only feasible option at first, they

---

98   Gianpietro Petriglieri, Susan Ashford, and Amy Wrzesniewski, "Thriving in the Gig Economy," *Harvard Business Review*, March-April 2018, https://hbr.org/2018/03/thriving-in-the-gig-economy.

turned out to be a good model, balancing human happiness with the need for employment.

In addition, for many diverse populations, including women and people with disabilities, work is only one part of their lives. The rest of their time is occupied by other pressing responsibilities or even just the time-consuming challenge of caring for themselves. And for many people from other cultures, the significance of work itself differs from the typical American perspective. Rather than forming the majority of one's identity, it's about making money to sustain oneself and one's family. It's a means to an end, not the end itself.

All of these circumstances are at odds with the structure of many powerful technology companies, which offer everything from meals and snacks to dry cleaning to create an environment such that workers don't ever have to go home. That culture might be amenable for someone who has no other responsibilities, but it's certainly not optimal for someone caring for a family or managing other needs. People may be excited about the in-office perks when they join an organization in their early twenties, but their priorities are likely to change as they get older.

To reap the beneficial insights of a diverse workforce, companies need to think about how they'll evolve to accommodate those with varied obligations. If we study those who have previously been excluded from corporate environments—such as women, people with disabilities, and aging employees—we can develop an employment model that better serves everyone. Their work-life integration will give us a glimpse of what employees will want, and demand, in the future.

In the spring of 2017, I was invited to join a Silicon Valley-based think tank called Innovation for Jobs (i4j). It is an organization working on this very issue. Cofounded and cochaired by David Nordfors and

Vinton Cerf, one of the "fathers of the internet" and chief internet evangelist for Google, i4j's goal is to "redirect AI to create good jobs for most people" and create a People-Centered Economy, or PCE. In this model, "people make themselves valuable by helping others make themselves worthy. When one earns more, others earn more, too and the economy grows."[99] This thinking aligns directly with Authentic Inclusion, in that everyone has value to add and a role to play in making the world better for us all.

With the knowledge that companies will increasingly be called upon to help make the world better for everyone, it's time for all of us to think about our sense of purpose. Consumers and workers want more from their products and their environment, and the most successful companies will do their best to meet the growing demand for personalization.

At the same time, we can't forget that humans are at the core of personalization, and that means ensuring that we don't alienate anyone in the process, whether it's through the data we collect or our expectations of the people doing the work. Cultivating a diverse group of design partners when it comes to developing products and services or creating experiences—professional and personal—will help. The next step is to truly operationalize human-first thinking, building it into everything we do.

---

99 "About i4j," Innovation for Jobs, accessed November 8, 2018, https://i4j.info/about/#forum.

CHAPTER 8
Taking Action to Impact Prosperity and Longevity: Authentic Inclusion by Design

W hen I retired from IBM to start my own consultancy, I knew I was taking on the challenge of being an independent player in the accessibility and inclusion space. I was giving up my bully pulpit as Chief Accessibility Officer with IBM to chart my own course. There would be new alliances and partnerships to forge as I continued to follow my purpose, though I was unsure of exactly how they would evolve.

Soon after I launched, I encountered an unexpected opportunity that was linked to the last customer event I had before my retirement from IBM in June 2016. I had spoken at the International Women's Forum World Cornerstone Conference in Tel Aviv in the spring of that year. The International Women's Forum (IWF) is an invitation-only group of high-powered women who are dedicated to advancing women's leadership around the world. The aim of the conference was to address significant societal issues, including technology, cybersecurity, and gender equality, particularly in a city "known for its constant change, fast-paced growth, and technological progress."[100]

My breakout session, titled "Rethinking Ability," focused on the importance of developing accessibility technology, which ultimately benefits the general population. "If you build accessibility thinking into your design, then you make your technology that much better. CXOs and investors need to see tech developed for the disabled as an avenue for more efficient machines for everybody," I told the audience.[101]

Dana Born, a retired brigadier general in the US Air Force, codirector of the Harvard Kennedy School's Center for Public Leadership, and chair of the Massachusetts chapter of the IWF, was in the audience, and later invited me to join the organization. I was honored by this invitation but didn't really appreciate what it meant until I heard why I was being nominated. Dana recognized that my knowledge, work, and experience in accessibility directly aligned with the IWF's mission, as well as with the charge for greater diversity in business overall. The way the members of the IWF acknowledged my value and welcomed me with open arms created an immediate sense of belonging. I knew that I would have the full support of this extraordinary group as I set out to write the next chapter in my career.

My experience with IWF over these last two years has been a natural extension of my work at IBM with the aging and people with disabilities. The fundamentals of Authentic Inclusion apply to any and every diversity group, including one of which I am now a member: women business leaders over age fifty. I recently gave a talk at a meeting

---

100 Viva Sarah Press, "International Women's Forum in Tel Aviv," Israel21c, May 18, 2016, https://www.israel21c.org/international-womens-forum-in-tel-aviv/.
101 Gedalyah Reback, "International Women's Forum Gives a Platform to Assistive Technology at Israel Confab," Geektime, accessed November 6, 2018, https://www.geektime.com/2016/05/23/international-womens-forum-gives-a-platform-to-assistive-technology-at-israel-confab/.

of the newly established New York City-based nonprofit Amazing Community, an organization "transforming [the] narrative about aging and innovation by redefining inclusive workplaces and equipping women 50+ to thrive in them."[102] I have also spoken at several conferences organized by Lesbians Who Tech, a group that is working to increase the visibility of lesbian technologists, grow the number of women in general working in technology, and build stronger networks within the technology community.[103] These are just a few examples of what Authentic Inclusion looks like in action, making space for everyone with the knowledge that we all have value to add.

In this chapter, we'll focus on the *how*. Incorporating Authentic Inclusion into business—and into society at large—requires three major elements: making Authentic Inclusion part of our mission on an individual level; operationalizing it through technology, policy, and practices; and taking action. While we've touched on each of these aspects throughout the book, here we'll delve a bit deeper and cover the steps necessary to take Authentic Inclusion from a corporate ideal to a core practice.

UPHOLDING OUR RESPONSIBILITY AS INDIVIDUALS

The route to transform our culture begins with individuals. Everyone in our society has the responsibility to work toward Authentic Inclusion in all of his or her roles—as citizens, customers, workers, and employers. Every decision we make and interaction we have is an opportunity to understand someone else's perspective more clearly, and to recognize its worth. If each of us makes a commitment to do that—one that is driven by authenticity and a human-first approach,

---

102 "About Us," Amazing Community, accessed November 4, 2018, http://amazing. community/comunity-resources/.

103 "About Lesbians Who Tech," Lesbians Who Tech, accessed November 8, 2018, https:// lesbianswhotech.org/about/.

not compliance or quotas—we'll be able to move the dial toward a better world for all.

FOR EXECUTIVES

Purposeful thinking and action are crucial for the executives who determine the course and priorities of their organizations. We understand all too well that, as we move up the ladder and take on more decision-making responsibilities, the questions that come across our desks get more complex. In addition, our society's growing challenges are increasingly reflected in our companies' policies and processes, and members of the senior leadership team are frequently called upon to make decisions rooted in broader cultural issues—like education of the future or employing people with disabilities. For topics like these, there's no formula. You can't simply measure input and output and generate a perfect answer.

This challenge is compounded by the fact that many of our decisions have a long-term impact. The ultimate outcome won't be evident in weeks, months, or quarters. Instead, we're essentially placing buoys in the sea, ones that will guide the actions of our companies—and society at large—for years to come. And often, the buoys themselves will be the only indication that we're headed in the right direction.

Being mindful of our impact can drive better decisions that ultimately serve our purpose and our companies' success. A strong sense of purpose—one that is rooted in authenticity—drives better and more consistent decisions. And the members of your organization will be inspired to follow your lead. As Michael Fieldhouse, then-program executive for the Dandelion Program at HPE—a highly effective employment initiative for people with autism—says, "Culture comes from the top. It is up to us within leadership teams to define and enact the attitudes that make people feel empowered."[104]

In fact, it was the involvement of executive team and government officials that made the Dandelion Program possible. They recognized that people on the autism spectrum often have exceptional abilities that can contribute to an organization's success, including extraordinary focus, memory skills, and the ability to notice errors and patterns that most neurotypical people would miss. In addition, they were committed to addressing the fact that, despite these special skills, people with autism are often underemployed. In Australia, where the program launched, the employment rate for those with autism is higher than 85 percent.[105]

With leadership support, the team worked with advocacy groups like Autism South Australia to establish the program, which placed people with autism in software testing roles in Australia's Department of Human Services. According to Fieldhouse, the program's goals are multifold: "to transcend social differences in order to deliver better services to customers and improve the company's competitive advantage (via a great example of inclusion), while generating big benefits for program participants and Australian society."[106]

The leaders' advocacy paid off. The program is exceeding its productivity targets, and participants are doing work of the highest quality. There is also major potential for growth. A PricewaterhouseCoopers report estimated that if a program like this one employed just 101 people (the original cohort included forty participants) and operated for twenty years, the benefit to the country would total

---

104 Michael Fieldhouse, "Why 'People Innovation' Is the Most Exciting Development of All," LinkedIn, November 6, 2016, https://www.linkedin.com/pulse/why-people-innovation-most-exciting-development-all-fieldhouse/.
105 Michael Fieldhouse, "Why the HPE Dandelion Program Is Now a Harvard Business School Case Study," LinkedIn, October 12, 2016, https://www.linkedin.com/pulse/why-hpe-dandelion-program-now-harvard-business-school-fieldhouse/.
106 Fieldhouse, "Why the HPE Dandelion Program."

$425 million.[107]

Those in leadership positions have a tremendous opportunity to enact innovative and productive programs like this one. When we are proactive about inclusion by seeking out diverse voices and committing to incorporating their feedback into our corporate strategies, we all reap the benefits.

FOR MANAGERS AND FRONT-LINE EMPLOYEES

Those who don't hold senior roles can also do their part to lead their organizations toward a more inclusive future. Based on my own executive experience, I know how easy it is to become isolated by a heavy workload and mounting responsibilities—and lose track of one's purpose in the process. Those of us who aren't in the C-suite but are in the management ranks can help by finding opportunities in the business setting to share our team's opinions, and perhaps most important, to encourage our employees to be themselves. You may be surprised to learn just how much the senior leaders of your organization appreciate your effort to represent your team's diverse insights and perspectives.

At every stage of my career, whether as an individual contributor or as a manager, I encountered members of the majority—white, American men—who were willing to hear me out when I had an idea to share or an insight to offer. Granted, I have had to do my part to make the communication a two-way street or facilitate the engagement, but authentic leaders do include diverse employees as part of their strategy to promote the longevity of their companies. They also want employees who can drive profits, and if you're different in some way, they could be looking for your talent and perspective to help the organization continue to move forward.

---

107 Fieldhouse, "Why 'People Innovation' Is the Most Exciting Development."

THE IMPACT OF ORGANIZATIONAL STRUCTURE

Once we embrace Authentic Inclusion personally, the next step is to make it into an organizational priority. We've established that accessibility is no longer optional; it is *integral*. Accessibility should be viewed alongside privacy and security as necessary to the infrastructure of any legitimate company.

System metrics like availability, reliability, and serviceability have been among these priorities before technology played such a personal role in all of our lives: *Can the system stay up without interruption? Is it easy to repair?* Today, there are additional concerns surrounding privacy and security that speak to tech's more personalized quality, and these factors are given great attention from day one and integrated at every level and stage of organizational development. Because we're talking about more than just hardware when we consider current infrastructure—with additional considerations about the human-facing aspects of products, services, and apps and the data they collect and protect—accessibility should be incorporated in a similar manner. Now that the user experience and consumer interactions are part of the mix, accessibility is a must. Like an elevator in a skyscraper, it should be part of the blueprint.

Doing this well often requires a change in perspective. The best organizations are innovative, and when inclusion is a key part of that innovation, businesses can leverage it to set themselves apart. This way of thinking is inherently different. And as a result, inclusion efforts will be more authentic, sustainable, and successful. IBM's decision to house its accessibility work within its research sector is a perfect example. With this structural setup, the company demonstrated its belief that inclusion is a key component of innovation and led in the development of accessible tech.

Similarly, in Chapter 6, we covered the importance of taking diversity and inclusion from an HR mandate to a business imperative that is addressed by every department and individuals at every level of the company—from the top down. Once we elevate inclusion solely from an HR practice into the business realm, the difference in perspective reveals its market potential.

This begins with the head of the organization conveying his or her commitment to Authentic Inclusion—not as an HR initiative or a corporate social responsibility statement, but as a fundamental business imperative. When leaders establish Authentic Inclusion as a key part of their business models, then the operating units within their companies—product, services, sales, marketing, communications, and others—will digest and integrate it in the same way, with general managers internalizing the message and relaying it to their teams for real action.

Incorporating an inclusion-based objective that is tied to business strategies and outcomes, from legal to product development and sales and marketing, can also help set the tone. Further, these objectives can be integrated and made visible in all of the organization's processes. For instance, if the vice president of communications is pushing out a promotional video, captioning could make it usable for people who can't hear it. If the claims processing department is creating a form that customers can fill out online, it can be made compatible with different assistive technologies so blind or low-vision customers can complete the form with ease. And when the CIO rolls out a new workplace email system, he or she has the opportunity to choose or develop a fully accessible system that every employee can use effectively. All these decisions can then be integrated into a management process so the institution can track its progress and create a closed-loop system to resolve any issues or challenges. In other words, manage authentic inclusion as you would any kind of business.

DEVELOP ACCESSIBILITY POLICY AND GOVERNANCE

Businesses can also engage in proactive thinking: rather than reacting on a case-by-case basis, consider building systems that can accommodate diverse needs before the request arises. The good news is you don't have to start from scratch. There are numerous advocacy groups that, along with technology companies—many of which we've discussed in this book—have created standards and best practices on this topic. If you choose to look for them, they're out there.

These concerns usually were not raised to the strategic level in the past because they were not viewed as being worthy of strategy. But once you can flip the switch and begin developing a more inclusive culture, all of the tools to craft it are there for the taking. You can begin by establishing an internal policy and external statement on your current accessibility work and your plans for the future.

And you don't have to wait until you've made significant strides; you can create an internal statement and external policy as soon as you decide on your accessibility plan. The goal here is not so much about listing accomplishments as it is about setting the tone for employees, customers, and clients. The policy provides employees with insight on the company's position on accessibility—expressing that it is a core value—and clarifies each person's accountability in helping to create an accessible workplace. Meanwhile, the statement informs clients and customers that accessibility is a priority within your organization and explains the steps being taken to advance the organization's goals in that realm.[108] It's never too early to put together these pieces because no matter the stage of your accessibility efforts, both employees and customers will appreciate knowing that you are taking steps to achieve a more inclusive environment.

---

108 "When and How to Write an Accessibility Statement and Policy [Policy]," UsableNet, August 27, 2018, https://blog.usablenet.com/when-and-how-to-write-an-accessibility-statement-and-policy-blog?hs_amp=true.

The W3C Web Accessibility Initiative offers a wealth of information on writing accessibility policies and statements, ensuring that other organizational processes align with these efforts, and creating an accessible website. For more information, head to www.w3.org.

EMBODY A SET OF CORE CHARACTERISTICS

Of course, developing a statement and policy is just a small piece of the puzzle. When determining the organizational aspects that make an organization truly inclusive, we can look to the Business Disability Forum, a United Kingdom-based nonprofit that helps businesses successfully employ and do business with people with disabilities. The Business Disability Forum has identified a set of common characteristics that make organizations "disability smart," with holistic policies and best practices to support people with disabilities. They found that organizations leading the way in accessibility have four characteristics in common:

- They understand how disability affects every aspect of the organization, not just individual issues, such as physical structures or recruitment.

- They proactively address any issues or barriers that limit everyone's ability to participate, whether they are employees, clients, or customers.

- They operate on an individual level, making adjustments for every person who needs them, and often ensure there is a system in place to regularly meet these needs.

- They don't make assumptions about abilities at large based on a particular impairment or diagnosis.[109]

---

109 Brendan Roach and Lucy Ruck, "Tackling Disability As a Global Business Issue," Business Disability Forum, YouTube video, 49:00, October 11, 2018, https://www. youtube.com/watch?v=v7t23z_0U7g.

These characteristics can serve as guidelines, helping you identify the programs and policies that will enable you to achieve Authentic Inclusion and build them in from the ground up.

EMBED INCLUSION IN YOUR TALENT STRATEGY TODAY

One aspect of inclusion that is of particular importance—and urgency—is talent. We covered the many benefits of hiring diverse talent in Chapter 5, but this becomes all the more pressing in today's current employment climate. As of August 2018, the US had 7.1 million job openings, the highest rate of open positions since the US Labor Department began tracking it in 2000.[110] Companies who have inclusion as part of their talent strategy can capitalize on new and different types of talent to close the gap.

As an added bonus, diverse hires will also be loyal and dedicated because those who are not part of the mainstream—such as myself—know when companies are genuinely interested in what they can contribute. In turn, they work for the company, not just a paycheck.

There is also a multiplier effect. When a company establishes itself as being interested in hiring top talent with different abilities, it attracts more highly skilled candidates who embrace those values. We've seen similar outcomes in many of the examples we've already discussed. Think back to IBM Brazil's ability to land a government grant and bring in leading researchers to run its project on employment and disability based on its reputation, as well as Deloitte's study revealing that 39 percent of employees would move to an organi-

---

110 Heather Long, "America Has a Record 7.1 Million Job Openings, Making It an Especially Advantageous Time to Ask for a Raise," *Washington Post*, October 16, 2018, https://www.washingtonpost.com/business/2018/10/16/america-has-record-million-job-openings-making-it-an-especially-advantageous-time-ask-raise/?noredirect=on&utm_term=.63a33d34b82d.

zation with more inclusive practices.[111] These are the kinds of big-picture items to think about when developing an inclusion strategy.

ADDRESS PROCUREMENT POLICIES

In addition to hiring employees with different backgrounds, experiences, and abilities, companies can also evaluate their procurement strategy. The US government is committed to contracting with diverse organizations that prioritize accessibility, and other organizations can benefit from adopting similar practices—ensuring that internal efforts and values are mirrored in vendor relationships.

Consider making it a priority to partner with women-, minority-, and veteran-owned businesses as well as those helmed by people with disabilities to ensure your employees, clients, customers, and other stakeholders know where you stand when it comes to prioritizing diversity. IBM was one of the first companies to work with Disability:IN (aka USBLN), an organization whose mission is to "promote disability inclusion by heightening awareness, advising corporations and sharing proven strategies for including people with disabilities in the workplace, supply chain, and marketplace," and was a founding member of numerous disability-owned business supplier initiatives.[112] In doing so, we invested in these businesses, made diversity sourcing a priority, and encouraged others to do the same.

---

111 Deloitte, "The Inclusion Imperative: Redefining Leadership," *Wall Street Journal*, September 4, 2018, https://deloitte.wsj.com/cio/2018/09/04/the-inclusion-imperative-redefining-leadership/https://deloitte.wsj.com/cio/2018/09/04/the-inclusion-imperative-redefining-leadership/.

112 "Who We Are," Disability:IN, accessed November 13, 2018, https://disabilityin.org/who-we-are/.

TO MEASURE INCLUSION EFFECTIVELY, USE A HUMAN-FIRST APPROACH

A different approach to inclusion also requires a different set of metrics. Determining the success of inclusion efforts based on employee demographics doesn't provide a complete picture; benchmarking other achievements helps determine whether employees have the tools to drive results. When I was Chief Accessibility Officer, I was measuring how accessible our products were and whether our teams had the skills to design accessible experiences. We still tracked our progress in terms of diversity, but we also measured the speed of innovation, the progression of our products and services, and our engagement with customers. Deviating from typical measurements can keep companies' focus on the bigger picture and help them gauge the human impact of their work.

Companies—especially large ones—can also benefit from an organizing body, like an accessibility center, working to ensure the entire organization is prioritizing accessibility through these and other methods. For example, the center could coordinate the engagement of senior management and unit leaders of each group on accessibility topics and create consistent operational interactions, with scheduled reviews to discuss the company's accessibility imperative and additional ways to operationalize it within various functions. These kinds of efforts and actions will ring true to employees and reflect an organization's authentic commitment to diversity and inclusion.

THE TIME IS NOW

As we consider the personal responsibility and operational aspects inherent in Authentic Inclusion, it's also important to recognize the pressing nature of these imperatives. The time is now. We've established time and again that technology is accelerating at such an incredible speed—and serving so many purposes in our lives—that participation is no longer nice to have; it's essential, and it has to begin today.

Moreover, with the knowledge that we are all likely to experience disability in some form or another thanks to aging, and that diversity touches all of our lives in one way or another, it behooves us to address the problems that will inevitably affect us, whether they are political, economic, or social. And to truly reach all customers—the individuals who make up the world—we need to tackle some of the complex and thorny problems plaguing society today. With the operational speed, efficiency, and insights that are often at the fingertips of businesses, many profit-driven operations are actually in the best position to solve some of these issues.

The demographic we're discussing is not a "them," it's an "us." When we put in the work to understand each other's perspectives and make a world that can serve all of us better, our present and future selves—and our companies and bottom lines—will see the difference.

Part of this is due to the fact that inclusive thinking requires us to incorporate multiple modes to account for different needs and abilities that hold benefits for everyone. Our ability to profit is no exception. As we become more agile, with multiple routes to problem solving and operations, we can respond to the market and generate more returns. Put simply, it's time to apply operational efficiency to human topics like diversity and authenticity. Doing so will harmoniously align principle, purpose, and profit for real longevity. I know because I've experienced it firsthand.

Over the course of my career, I have witnessed so many displays of Authentic Inclusion and its power—from the professors who approved my application to study in America, to Frank Friedersdorf, who gave me my first job, and the thousands of people I met at IBM and beyond. Through the opportunities I received, I was able to tap into my purpose and work toward creating a better work environment for the company's employees and a better product for every customer.

I learned so much as an executive in numerous capacities—from marketing and sales to business development and research innovation—and, of course, as Chief Accessibility Officer. Through my personal experiences, my work at IBM, and the connections I made to people in the disability community, I know Authentic Inclusion works. It is not only the right thing to do but also essential to surviving and thriving as technology continues to advance at an incredible pace.

Sharing my knowledge more broadly and helping companies and institutions do this crucial work is the next phase for me. Through advisory work, speaking engagements, and strategic partnerships, my company, FrancesWestCo, aims to influence leaders, impact businesses, and inspire organizational transformation. I hope you'll join me.

ACKNOWLEDGMENTS

I would like to express my most sincere thanks to:

John Kemp, President and CEO of The Viscardi Center, an incredibly inspiring individual who has shared his personal story and his wisdom about the disability industry with me throughout the years.

To all the IBM executives who supported my work throughout my career and the IBM colleagues who worked with me to make a difference, especially the individuals in the IBM Accessibility organization who epitomize Authentic Inclusion in everything they do, every day.

To two very special ex-IBMers:

Chris Caine, President and CEO at Mercator XXI, LLC, who has been my mentor all these years. His trust and confidence in me gave me the direction and inspiration to continue the accessibility journey.

Kathleen Delgado, who was the Accessibility Marketing Manager in IBM Research and is now my colleague at FrancesWestCo. Without her knowledge, guidance, and expert advice at every turn, I would not have had the belief that I could write and finish this book.

To all the companies and organizations I have had the honor to serve as a board member, member, or advisor, and who taught me everything about disability, accessibility, and diversity:

Aira https://aira.io

American Association of People with Disabilities (AAPD)
https://www.aapd.com

Assistive Technology Industry Association (ATIA)
https://www.atia.org

Chinese Disabled Persons' Federation (CDPF)
https://en.wikipedia.org/wiki/
China_Disabled_Persons%27_Federation

Disability:IN https://disabilityin.org

Inclusite https://www.inclusite.com

Innovation for Jobs (i4j) https://i4j.info

International Women's Forum (IWF) http://iwforum.org

Global Initiative for Inclusive ICTs (G3ict) http://www.g3ict.org

Knowbility https://knowbility.org

Mercator XXI https://www.mercatorxxi.com

My Blind Spot https://myblindspot.org

National Braille Press (NBP) http://www.nbp.org

Ruh Global https://www.ruhglobal.com

Shenzhen Information Accessibility Association http://siaa.org.cn

SourceAmerica https://www.sourceamerica.org

University of Massachusetts, Boston, and Medical School

https://www.umb.edu, https://www.umassmed.edu

US International Council on Disabilities (USICD)
http://www.usicd.org/template/index.cfm

The Viscardi Center https://www.viscardicenter.org

World Information Technology and Services Alliance (WITSA)
https://witsa.org

World Institute on Disability (WID) https://wid.org

World Wide Web Consortium (W3C) https://www.w3.org/WAI

Zhejiang University (ZJU) https://www.zju.edu.cn/english

CPSIA information can be obtained
at www.ICGtesting.com
Printed in the USA
BVHW040827250319
542838BV00009B/13/P